HERE I AM.

Finding Oneself Through

Healing and Letting Go

Cataloguing in Publication Data
O'Meara, Mark Linden, 1958 -
  Here I am

  Includes bibliographical references and index.
  ISBN 0-9680459-1-X

  1.Personality and Emotions. 2. Self-realization.
3. Personality change. I Title.
BF698.9.E45O43 1997   158.1   C97-910465-3

Published by
Soul Care Publishing,
1733 H Street, Suite 330-965
Blaine WA 98230-5106
(604) 878-0487

Cover design and artwork by Joanne Probyn

Excerpts from the *Fundamentals of Co-Counseling Manual* re-
printed with permission of Harvey Jackins and Rational Island
Publishers, PO Box 2081, Main Office Station, Seattle, Wash-
ington, 98111, USA
Lyrics to *"Cry (If you want to)"* reprinted with the permission of
Casey Scott and Signal Songs/Tainjo Thang (ASCAP) All Rights
Reserved/Used by Permission
Excerpts from *It Could Never Happen to Me* reprinted with per-
mission of M.A.C. Publishing, 1850 High Street, Denver, Colo-
rado

Printed in Canada

About the Author

A warm, personable lecturer, author/educator Mark Linden O'Meara relates his knowledge and life experience in transitions, letting go, and healing in a thought provoking, nurturing and personal manner.

In completing his Masters Degree in Education (Counselling Psychology) Mark is near the completion of a powerful transition that stemmed from challenging life experiences that resulted in the creation of the book *"Here I Am: Finding Oneself through Healing and Letting Go"* - a comprehensive guide to working through emotions, rediscovering oneself, developing healthier relationships and experiencing a healthier lifestyle.

After completing his Bachelor of Management Science in Information Systems, Mark began working as a consultant. At the same time Mark experienced a number of losses that, as one mentor noted, fundamentally changed his outlook and sense of self.

This trying period resulted in the recollection of painful childhood memories as well as the need to heal from these and other events. Through the use of self-expression, emotional catharsis, and challenging his beliefs about himself and others, he has experience a reconnection with joy and a deepening of his friendships.

As a result of these changes Mark has experienced significant personal growth and satisfaction. Mark has been thoroughly enjoying his teaching experience at the community college level for over 5 years, has presented at professional conferences, and has been featured on radio and TV.

Dedication...

This book is dedicated to all the people who came into my life when I needed them, to provide support, encouragement, to teach me a lesson I needed to learn, or to tell me the name of a book I needed to read. Without them, my healing process wouldn't have been possible, nor the creation of this book. And to my parents, who gave me life.

Special thanks to the following people who helped me greatly in the creation of this book: Theresa Khidir-Lethbridge for proofreading and editing of the initial manuscript; Sylvia Arnold for editing suggestions, proofreading and encouragement; Nancy Cain for providing valuable feedback; Joan Boxwell and Kelly Davidson for proofreading and editing of the final drafts of the manuscript; Bruce Messecar for encouragement and help in understanding my issues; Helen Bourgeois for support, understanding, and long distance calls; Cathy Pothier for encouragement and believing in me; and Donna Ferguson for, among other things, her sense of humor.

Mark O'Meara, June 12th, 1997

Table of Contents

Introduction

In our quest to heal from troubles many of us have been told to "let go". Although the advice seems appropriate, many of us do not know how to let go. The actual process of letting go is something we may not have experienced, and we may therefore need to learn how to achieve this. I believe that letting go is a complicated process and that there are many factors that facilitate or hinder this process. While much of this book focuses on the nature of letting go, it also focuses on the nature of healing, for by learning about the process of healing, we learn the process of letting go.

In this book I hope to describe the notions, ideas, techniques and attitudes that facilitate letting go and healing. In this process, you too can learn and experience the benefits of getting in touch with your emotional self and begin to develop attitudes that will promote healing. In doing so, we can become less fearful of our emotions and learn to let go of them. We can learn to develop healthier emotional attitudes and behaviors that will affect our relationships and friendships. It is also about discovering or expanding our rainbow of emotions and creative talents that exist within ourselves, learning to nurture ourselves and beginning to promote healthy thinking and behavior. This book, therefore, is also about better communication, closer relationships, greater joy, and a greater sense of connection with our selves and with others. All of these things are tied together in our ability to express, communicate and resolve our emotions.

Until a few years ago, my life was greatly affected by a backlog of emotion. A difficult childhood as well as a number of losses, combined with the avoidance of my emotions, led me to a troubled state of crisis. I was fatigued, isolated and my thinking was troubled. A friend confided to me that no matter how hard I tried to have a good time, it seemed that something was pulling me down. I was in a great deal of emotional pain, yet could not communicate this to others, nor could I admit it to myself. I kept myself very busy, sometimes compulsively, yet even though I realized I needed to slow down, could not. Although emotionally wound up, I was also extremely numb to my own feelings. I have been told that I gave the impression I wanted to be left alone even though my heart longed for companionship. Most of my obsession with projects and my at times irrational behavior were the means of avoiding my feelings. It is from this state however, that I moved to a sense of serenity and connectedness with others. This change came about as I learned to deal with my emotions more effectively and challenged the beliefs held within those emotions.

In the last few years I have learned a tremendous amount about the nature of emotions and what happens when they are suppressed. I have also read countless articles and papers regarding the effects of emotional, physical and sexual abuse of the lives of the victims. The incidence of addiction, depression and mental health problems are clearly linked to these distressing situations. However, we do not need to experience extreme traumatic events to end up being emotionally numb, out of touch with our feelings, and rationally impaired. Stressful life events, unsupportive family environments, or growing up in addictive or dependent families can lead to similar conditions.

Fortunately, I have experienced the reality that the effects of these traumas are not permanent and that healing can take place. Through some trial and error, the support of others, seemingly chance meetings with people, and reading the appropriate book at the appropriate time, I experienced a major shift in my emotional health. I have worked hard and diligently at getting in touch with my emotions, releasing them and healing. The work has paid off! I developed a much deeper understanding of myself, my past, and the emotions I was feeling in the present. In my healing process, I developed new friendships, changed careers, developed a healthier approach to myself and improved my decision making. I no longer long for companionship, but recognize what I have to offer and bring to others. My self-esteem has improved. I am more assertive, and I experience a greater degree of joy in my life.

I have learned that it is possible to safely express and resolve emotions and to heal emotional hurt and pain, and in doing so experience a sense of renewal and revitalization. I am now more energetic, have achieved better relationships and friend-ships, and definitely have greater joy and excitement in my life. Friends tell me that I smile more often and that I walk taller. I no longer have a lingering sense of pain and weariness hanging over my shoulder! When issues arise, I am dealing mostly with the current situation rather than my emotional history. Without emo-tional baggage, others find it easier to communicate with me. When issues come up in a relationship, I can deal with them more effectively, having dealt with my past. Of course I still have dif-ficult days, but I have successfully resolved a great deal of what is commonly referred to as emotional baggage and have begun to live my life in the way that I believe is a dream come true. Sim-ply reminding myself of these improvements makes my day bet-ter!

Ironically, all of this growth came about after making a New Year's resolution to experience more joy in my life, yet it was through the facing of my troubles that brought about a greater sense of joy. In the three years following my New Year's resolu-tion, I have experienced a tumultuous period of change in my surroundings, social life and self knowledge. During this period I learned a great deal about the dynamics of releasing, letting go and healing. At first I believed that catharsis was enough. As I observed my own process, I quickly learned that changing one's beliefs and behavior were also necessary and that these aspects, as well as emotional expression, were intricately linked in very subtle ways. The ideas in this book have helped me tremendously. I hope to share those insights so that you and others may benefit from what I have learned and begin to experience more joy in your lives as I have.

The events that brought about the creation of this book seem humorous now that I look back. Originally I started to write a how-to book on buying a house! I rented a portable computer to do some writing at my brother's cottage; during the daytime I worked on a few projects around the cottage, and wrote during the quiet evening hours. My father had dug a well at our cottage years before. Each spring, pine needles and other debris would find their way into the well and an annual cleaning was required at the beginning of the cottage season. As I began this project, I noticed that my father had taken a number of shortcuts in building the foundation of rocks that lined the well. I ended up removing all the original work and rebuilding it from the bottom with a new and stronger foundation. This was so much like an analogy of what I had done in my own life that I wrote a short essay on the subject. Then I wrote another essay on another topic, and another and so on and so forth.

With my new goal of writing a book and having experienced a great deal of positive change, I wanted to ensure that I fully understood the process that I had moved through. I also wanted to identify the key elements that facilitated my healing process. In doing so, I believed that I could pass on valuable knowledge to others. And so I began writing, which in itself was positive and cathartic. I spent considerable time collecting information on the topics of healing, health, and resolving emotions in order to understand the process I went through. I searched for articles on the effects of emotional release. I also developed a collection of notes that I scribbled onto napkins, scraps of paper, match covers, and concert programs which were then transformed into a manuscript.

This book is the result of my healing process and describes what I have learned during that time. It is hoped that the information and techniques in this book will help you in your goal of emotional healing. In reading this book, I would like you to keep in mind that there is no right or wrong way to go about healing and letting go. Each of us are unique and therefore the techniques or solutions that you choose may be different from those someone else would choose. The images and experiences that you related to will also be unique. As a result, I have not included case studies in this book as it would not be possible to include the depth and subtleties of any one individual's experience. In reading about the ideas and techniques I present, I suggest that you examine your own life to see how they apply to you. Try to apply them in your own unique way to your own life and situation. I hope that you create your own experience from reading these pages.

In doing so, I believe that your emotional healing will allow you to feel more joy and to be more expressive. It will unlock your creativity and spontaneity and lead to better family relationships, friendships and a greater degree of understanding of yourself and others. One of the greatest challenges to which we can rise is healing ourselves. It is an act we do for ourselves that can have profound effects on our lives and our futures.

Emotional Training

The Child's Natural Expression

I am always amazed how a whole room of activity will come to a grinding stop when a newborn is brought into the room. Everyone stops what ever activity they are involved in and a collective "ooooohh!" fills the room! The same thing occurs when someone presents a collection of baby pictures. What is it that so strongly catches our attention? The next time you encounter such a situation, I suggest you study the facial expressions of a little one! You will likely notice the unrestrained expression of joy, discovery, and laughter on their little faces. If feeding or changing time is missed, or a parent leaves the room, you will quickly encounter the expression of pain, sadness and even anger.

Young children are exuberant and uninhibited in their emotional expression. In their faces we see the full range of emotions -from sadness and anger to joy and excitement -all within the space of a few moments. Their facial expressions clearly reflect their true emotional state -free of any emotional encumbrances. Except for children brought to term with substance or alcohol abuse, each child born into this world is, at birth, lovable and emotionally expressive and although the thinking processes have not been fully developed, the child is capable of developing rational thoughts and will develop the ability to reason. As humans we are born lovable, vital, vibrant, confident, emotional, loving and rational beings. This natural ability to be loved, to think clearly, and to reason clearly is what is sometimes referred to as our own "inherent nature". We are born with it; it is a natural state. In this sense we are all born equal.

Harvey Jackins, the founder of the re-evaluative counseling movement, writes in *Fundamentals of Co-counselling*:

"After being hurt, an infant will cry loudly and continuously and, if permitted to do so, will seem to recover from the hurt very quickly. After being frightened badly, an infant will scream and shake and perspire. After being angered, a yelling, vigorous tantrum will result, unless interfered with by others in the vicinity. A child, given friendly attention after an embarrassing situation, will talk and laugh about the experience spontaneously until the embarrassment is dissipated. These discharges - the crying, the trembling, the angry shouting, the laughter - are the ways in which human beings release the tensions which the experiences of hurt place upon them.

Apparently babies - given a chance - would keep themselves free from hurts simply by their natural discharge of painful emotion. In our culture, no baby gets very much of a chance because, with sympathy or with harshness, the discharge of painful emotion is interfered with and shut off so repeatedly that to shut it off becomes an automatic pattern accompanying the hurt."

In his book *Catharsis in Healing, Ritual and Drama*, T.J. Scheff suggests that as humans we are born with the innate ability to express emotions. As we progress through the years into adulthood, society trains us to suppress our emotional side, resulting in fewer genuine facial expressions and less spontaneity.

As a child begins to grow, he or she will experience day to day life events that will bring about emotional experiences. Although we may think of children as being carefree and living in a special fantasy world, children are faced with problems of their own. When they face these problems, they need to be listened to and helped in identifying their feelings just as adults do. Yet, how many of us have heard someone yelling "Stop it, stop it now or you will really have something to cry about!" While camping recently, I overheard a mother telling her daughter that the adults wouldn't like her if she continued to cry!

Due to the environment that the child grows up in, the child may be nurtured in expressing emotions or the child may be taught to curtail emotions. The nurturing of emotional expression will aid the child to maintain his or her inherent nature of rational thoughts and reason, and will continue to experience him or herself as lovable. In the event that the child's emotions are shamed, or that the child is taught to suppress emotions, the child's inherent nature will be clouded over with negative messages about him or herself.

If we have healthy emotional patterns of expression then, as events occur, we can examine them and express emotions accordingly. As adults, many of us have lost that connection between ourselves and the ability to identify and express our emotions. This is not something that usually happens overnight, but something that creeps up on us over a long period of time. In our childhood, teenage or adult years we may have been unsuspectingly taught to hide and suppress our emotions due to cultural expectations or due to a fear of being ridiculed by others. Quite often these were not formal lessons or directions, but messages we were given through the behavior of others. If we were angry, perhaps someone would walk away. If we were upset, perhaps someone ignored us. In some cases, emotions were simply not tolerated by others in our environment. We may have been told to stop crying or rewarded for stifling our feelings. In my particular case, I remember instances of stuffing down my feelings and being very fearful of letting anyone know how I was feeling. It was just too scary!

The negative messages that children receive about emotional expression are numerous and sometimes confusing. Quite often these messages are the result of the adult's inability to tolerate emotion in themselves rather than anything to do with the child's behavior. For most of us, the expression of emotions has decreased with age, however it is clear to me that the moderation of emotional expression appears to be a learned behavior rather than a biological or personality trait. The young baby mentioned earlier learns from its environment about the effects of displaying emotion. Many parents attempt to train their children to stop crying although this is changing. Children are often scolded, called crybabies, and are given negative messages about crying or expressing anger.

There is a positive movement in this area though, and not all is gloomy. Recently, while in a hardware store, I observed a young couple dealing with a young crying boy. Both the mother and father were actively participating in reassuring and encouraging the young child to express whatever was upsetting him.

They did not attempt to get him to stifle his tears but encouraged them! A few moments later, the cashier told the little boy "I'll give you a candy if you stop crying", to which his parents replied with a warm smile "Could he have the candy even if he continues crying?" The cashier smiled and gave the boy the candy while he continued to cry. This story reminds me of the fact that males in particular have been taught to repress crying, while females have been traditionally taught to repress anger. Perhaps we might consider the cost of rewarding children for stifling their emotions!

With regard to gender, there have been a number of differences in how boys and girls are treated with respect to emotional expression. These differences can not only bring about patterns of behavior, but can also generate gender stereotypes. While females are often thought of as being more emotionally expressive, I believe this to be a stereotype. Although crying is more prevalent among women, this may only be a factor of culture. It may not be a sign that women have a greater emotional capacity, but simply that the expression of emotion in males has been suppressed or trained out of them, while accepted for females.

Males in particular may be unable to express emotion simply due to societal expectations. Rarely do we see films or TV shows in which males cry. Typically, male crying has been identified as a sign of weakness resulting in males being fearful of expressing themselves. This is changing however, as society begins to learn that our emotions are a normal part of being human and as the roles of males and females change. While males have typically been stereotyped as non-expressive, this is not in fact the reality. We find many males openly discussing and expressing emotions in art, self-help groups and in close friendships. While some studies have shown that females will often score higher on adjustment tests, this may only be reflecting a greater willingness to accept the expression of emotion.

In a recent study of brain use patterns, it was shown that there is a biological basis for the difference in female and male behaviors. The study showed that on average, women are more inclined to exercise a portion of the lower brain that helps refine the way emotions are expressed. The author of the report, Ruben C. Gur, states that "Our findings do not answer the question of whether the differences are genetic or cultural in origin. After all, culture shapes the brain just as the brain shapes culture."

Regardless of gender, many people have learned various methods of expressing their emotions and many have developed methods of withholding or denying their emotions. In the course of writing this book, I have encountered numerous males and females who were experiencing emotional numbness and who were looking for ways to connect with themselves. One should not generalize about these gender issues. Both males and females learn to hide their anger or provide a smile when they greet someone who has hurt them. All are behaving in ways that block or hide their true emotions. This decline in expression does have its price. These people are all robbing themselves of the value of emotional expression.

As in my case, the suppressing of emotions often leads to greater problems. Many children, adolescents and adults have suffered through painful experiences such as abandonment, emotional or sexual abuse. As a result, their ability to function in other spheres of their life has been impaired. At the heart of every addiction lies a wounded soul. The key to long term resolution of addiction and other destructive behavior is found by developing new ways to handle anxiety, by accessing and resolving the underlying problem, and by developing greater self-esteem. Helping to increase self awareness by identifying and disclosing the nature of the emptiness in the soul and releasing the pent-up emotional pain assists in giving up the addiction or compulsive behavior.

In many self-help programs, the process of hitting bottom, and subsequent release of emotions within a spiritual context, is a common occurrence among participants. The reappearance of positive feelings, allowing them to experience the joys of life, have been observed and documented. While it cannot be medically explained, it often occurs in life and is considered a mystery of spiritual phenomenon. Perhaps this re-experiencing of emotions fosters a connection with others, for emotions are the basis of the strongest form of communication we possess.

Emotional Myths

Typically, emotions have been labeled as either positive (such as joy and happiness) or negative (such as sadness, anger and depression). Love and contentment have been viewed as the opposite of anger and rage, while joy and happiness have been viewed as opposites of sadness and depression.

Some of these views are founded on old belief systems. Some of us believe that to get angry at someone means that we do not love the person, or that happiness is a sign of mental health. Furthermore, very few people have learned to discern the difference between anger and aggression. The negative aspects of aggression have mistakenly been confused with anger. Anger is equally an important form of communication in relationships as love. To express anger appropriately is not a sign of disrespect or a lack of love. When someone expresses anger it is usually because they care enough about the relationship to express the need that is not being met.

Perhaps we need to re-evaluate the traditional scale and begin to view emotions as neither positive or negative but simply as a reflection of our beliefs and the events that are occurring in our lives. A more appropriate and healthy scale of emotions would involve classifying depression, aggression, anxiety, rage and love as states of mind rather than emotions. Anger, fear, joy, and happiness occur in everyday life and are not necessarily negative or positive. Each has their own unique value in our lives and without one we cannot experience the others.

One of the most common myths about emotions is that we believe we have the ability to selectively block out certain emotions. We tend to believe that we can avoid anger, yet still feel love; that we can block out sadness and still feel joy. Perhaps we may have numbed out some of our emotions and still feel a degree of love and joy. In fact, our capacity for joy and love is limited when we suppress our emotions and build up tension. The truth about emotions is that we do not truly have the ability to selectively block out only a spectrum of emotions. If we block sadness or anger we also end up limiting our ability to feel joy.

One of the benefits of working on our emotional healing is

that we generally find a greater capacity for joy and for sharing in our lives once we begin to resolve our emotional baggage. A "put-on" smile is replaced with a more genuine smile that comes from the heart. A greater degree of closeness develops with others as our thinking becomes clearer and as we become less fearful of others discovering or opening up our pain. The path to joy is found by facing our pain and accepting that life is difficult. Life is a series of ups and downs. Perhaps a measurement of mental health is our ability to experience the full range of emotions that occur as a result of events in our lives.

Emotional Role Models

In recalling my childhood, I remember a number of adults who impacted my own emotional well being. Some of them listened and encouraged the expression of my ideas, while others were too lost in their own problems and discomfort and provided discouragement. In my adult life, and particularly in 12-step groups, I encountered people who were nurturing and supportive. All of these people have been role models in some way or another to me - some positively and some negatively. These role models can have a tremendous impact on our emotional well being and awareness.

Patterns of emotional expression or non-expression are developed by observing the behavior of our emotional role models. These role models may be parents, teachers, extended family, scout leaders, daycare workers, or anyone who has contact with us. Our family emotional patterns can greatly influence our ease or unease regarding the display of emotions. Some families may encourage emotional expression and creativity but many families do not tolerate it. Some may accept emotional expression in children but not tolerate it with adults. With many families the rules are not clearly spelled out in directives, but are defined by the examples of others. My own father never gave any indication as to what he was feeling. He was impossible to read. Questioning him about how he was doing was treated as an intrusion. While most people appreciate the concern of others, my father's behavior led me to believe that asking questions was inappropriate. For myself, this replicated behavior pattern appeared to others as disinterest. Once I learned that questioning was OK and normal, and began practicing it as a social skill, my social and work situation began to improve. I still have to catch myself sometimes though, and remember to ask how the other person is doing!

As described above, quite often the emotional maturity of the parents will greatly affect their ability to tolerate emotional expression in their children. If the parents have worked through issues and healed from their own losses, then they are more likely to encourage emotional expression and healing rather than hinder or shame the child for being emotional. Shame is experienced when we are given the message that we, rather than our behavior, are bad or inadequate. There is an important distinction between behavior and the individual. When a child behaves improperly, the child needs discipline and guidance, not shaming.

Often children are shamed for getting angry at their parents. Children get angry and have a right to express it, yet many parents fear this expression as a challenge to their authority. However, anger is a communication tool and can be a door opener to better communication. The expression of anger can facilitate feedback and expression of needs. True communication follows when we are emotionally expressive. If the parents have a great backlog of emotional issues, then true expression may be difficult due to a greatly enhanced fear of criticism.

Honest communication cannot occur if the parent is overwhelmed by self criticism and defeatist attitudes. In this case the child cannot feel free to express his or her self without fear of upsetting the parent. The child can then develop an improper responsibility for other peoples' feelings when it is the adult who has the emotional coping problems. The child will become fearful of expressing emotions due to the consequences and patterns that appear when communication is attempted with the emotionally clouded adult. An adult who experienced this type of childhood will need to learn that emotions can be expressed without causing harm or hurting others.

A great hindrance of emotional expression can occur when one or both of the parents assume a "peace at any cost" role. To avoid conflict, a parent may try to deal with issues by doing anything within their power to placate the parties with the conflict. This can be done by covering debts, by speaking to the parties individually, or by caretaking. This usually results in the issue being resolved but without any actual communication between the two. As a result, the emotions are not expressed and the parties do not learn to resolve their issues through communication and expression. This can lead to a fear of bringing up and confronting issues as adults.

Another factor that affects both adults and children is the perfect family image that many parents try to maintain. This results in the denial of family problems and making many topics off limits for discussion. Again, the lack of discussion and resolution of issues creates emotional tension and isolation in the family. This tension will manifest itself in the family behavior patterns unless an awareness of the habits is developed and worked on.

In many religious circles, showing anger towards God is considered sinful. While I used to fear my religious God, my sense of faith has truly changed. I now recognize that it is acceptable to get angry. At one point in the writing of this book I discovered that I had to move. While driving around searching for vacancy signs I looked up to the sky and said "It's my turn God. I've heard of people finding great places to live by chance. It's my turn to be helped out." Within five minutes of getting home, my phone rang. A friend called to say that due to a call from his former landlord, he knew of an apartment to rent. I took it immediately. It was literally a godsend -it is quiet, has lots of windows, nice fellow tenants and a spectacular view of sailboats on the water, parks, and snow-capped mountains.

Examining and identifying the behavior patterns of our role models, as well as our own habits that we have developed, is a necessary step in facilitating our own emotional awareness. The level of emotional acceptance in our role models may lead us to shut down emotionally or to be more expressive. Again, these patterns are learned behaviors. Healthier and more open patterns of expression can be learned to replace the old ineffective behaviors. The patterns we choose to develop and use end up shaping our choices in friends, careers, attitudes, and partners.

Can Others Make Me Feel?

One of the last areas to be discussed in this chapter is our responsibility for feelings. There are actually two questions or aspects to discuss. The first is whether or not someone can make another person feel a certain way. The second aspect is whether we should feel responsible for another person's feelings.

With respect to the first question, assertiveness training coaches would suggest that another person cannot make you feel a certain way. But I must ask whether this is realistic. If someone belittles us, shouts at us or even just sits and whines about how hopeless and negative their future is, it is difficult not to be impacted in some way. It is important for us to look at how we behave in these situations. Do we stick around, or do we assertively communicate our concerns. Does the other person listen or are they simply too abusive to be concerned about our feelings?

In the research world, it is recognized that the simple act of observing can impact study participants. My point is that in some situations, it is almost impossible to avoid being impacted by other people's behaviors. Relationships will affect you just as you will affect them. You and others do matter in some way or another. As adults, it is what we do when we are being impacted by another person, that results in control over our situation and therefore our feelings. Unfortunately, as children or perhaps at times in our adult lives, we were unable to effect the choices we would have liked to make.

What often comes into play are the beliefs and the judgments we have about ourselves that cause us to feel the emotions of shame, guilt or responsibility. Unfortunately, a child or teenager may have no situation other than his or her own family against which to compare or develop other belief systems. There is no fault in someone developing a sense of shame or guilt in a family situation that offers little or no healthy emotional and nurturing support. It is unfair to say that someone chose to feel that way. Evaluating these types of situations requires objective thinking. If we do not have other reference points, then we fall into a trap of believing the shaming authority.

I remember my father saying "if you don't make it home from the cottage by eleven then I'll be so worried that I won't be able to sleep." Am I responsible for my fathers' worry? No. What he was really saying was, "I do not take responsibility for my behavior. It is you who I will hold responsible for my feelings of worry." In this case, the worry is more of a behavior and my father's behavior reflects his inability to trust and his discomfort with his feelings. I have heard similar statements from others such as "if you don't come home for Christmas, it'll be ruined" or variations thereof. What is really being said in such situations is that the parent does not want to accept that their children have grown up and have their own lives, and perhaps the parent is unwilling to look at their own loneliness. The feelings of the parent are not examined but are ricocheted onto the children by suggesting that they are responsible for the emotions. Some adults make "you make me feel...." statements when another person is not doing what the parent asks. These are often not statements of disclosure, but are manipulative statements intended to change the choice of action or behavior of the other person.

One needs to recognize the distinction between the impact one's feelings have on others and the impact that one's behavior has on others. Our behavior can result in feelings in others, but we cannot control what those feelings will be, just as we cannot make someone love us, no matter how hard we try. Certainly, some behaviors will likely result in a greater respect between two individuals and a greater chance of being liked. But no one can be the sole creator of feelings in another person. The creation of a response in any individual requires the processing of communication. This process involves interpretation of messages created with an imprecise language, recalling similar experiences and examining one's beliefs. No one should hold us solely accountable for their feelings.

Of course, we need to be accountable for our behavior, but emotional ransom is a behavior not to be tolerated. Clearly, someone might tell us that if we left them, they'd feel hurt. We still need to be sensitive to the feelings of others, but we also need to consider our own needs and whether the statement is made for the purpose of communication or manipulation.

Clearly, some situations will likely evoke certain emotions and beliefs in us. If we were emotionally abused, then we will likely feel low self esteem and have difficulty trusting others. But as discussed later in the book, blaming does not help. When we understand the way we are, we are free to make choices and to heal. We can develop new attitudes, learn to trust and take responsibility for ourselves, given the understanding we have of the problem!

Our Emotional Habit Inventory

In understanding our own emotional habits, we can look back to our own habits and comfort level in expressing ourselves. In a book about adult children of alcoholics titled *It Could Never Happen to Me*, author Claudia Black provides a questionnaire that helps us to learn about our own history and current practices of emotional expression. By answering each question we can get a better understanding of our own emotional behavior inventory.

Answering these questions may take some reflecting and effort at remembering how things were. In addition, it is equally important to ask ourselves how we would answer these questions, regarding our current behavior. Have we carried any of those behaviors into our adulthood? In answering these questions, I realized that in most cases I was crying silently even though no one was around. I realized that this was a carry over from my childhood. Many times I cried myself to sleep, but silently so no one would know. By discovering this I gained a stronger sense of voice and expression which impacted my singing abilities.

How would you answer the questions below? Keep in mind that there are no right or wrong answers to this questionnaire.

1. When do you cry?
2. Do you ever cry?
3. Do you cry when alone?
4. Do you cry hard or do you cry slowly and silently?
5. Do you cry because people hurt your feelings?
6. Do you cry for no apparent reason?

7. Do others know when you cry?
8. Do others see you cry?
9. Do others hear you cry?
10. Do you let others comfort you when you cry?
11. Do you let others hold you?
12. Do you let them just sit with you?
13. What do you do to prevent yourself from crying?
14. How is your pattern as an adult different from that of a child?
15. What did you do with your tears as a child?
16. Did you cry?
17. Did others know you were crying?
18. Did you let others comfort you when you were crying?
19. What did you do to prevent yourself from crying?

Although the above questionnaire deals with crying, we need to examine our habits regarding joy and laughter as well. In addition to repressing crying as a child or adult, often we tend to repress our joy as well. Many families do not share in the joy of others. Repressing emotions is similar to turning down the volume on a stereo. The full range of sound is lowered in volume. Unlike current stereos which have numerous controls to shape the sound, we do not have the ability to selectively block out only certain emotions. If emotional repression is the norm in a family then it follows that joy and happiness will not be shared as well. The following questions can help you understand your past with respect to joy and happiness. Again, there are no right or wrong answers, but these questions will help in identifying factors that can contribute to or distract from our current enjoyment of life.

1. Did you experience joy in your family?
2. Did others express laughter?
3. Did others share your joy?
4. Were you laughed at or ridiculed for laughing or being spontaneous?
5. Was depression a major factor in the day to day life of a family member?

6. Do you feel comfortable laughing and expressing emotion as an adult?
7. Were you taught to feel guilty for having fun?
8. Were you very quiet?
9. Were you spontaneous?
10. Were you expressive?
11. As an adult do you express your creativity in some way?
12. Are you creative in your work?
13. Can you easily have fun or be silly?
14. Are you easy-going?
15. Do you let the child in you come out to play?
16. What makes you sad?
17. What makes you happy?

Fortunately, as humans we are able to effect change in our personal habits and behavior in relationships once we become aware of our patterns and emotional hurt. Once we are aware, we can slowly change our attitudes and behavior, through our own emotional healing work, to encourage emotional expression in our children. We can change the way we behave in our own families. We can do things differently than the way our parents did. The first step is awareness.

On Becoming Affectionate

One of the attributes of being human is our need for affection. This, of course, is not to be confused with sex, which unfortunately many people equate with affection. Each of us needs to be held, to be hugged and to be able to show our affection with others. We are healthier, both in mind and spirit, when we are able to experience the warmth of affection with another. Unfortunately, many people including myself, begin life in an environment where affection was not present. I do not remember my mother holding me, and I remember my father being cold and unresponsive when I was a child. As children, we learn from our role models. We tend to develop behaviors based on the modeling of the adults around us. If appropriate affection is shown between parents and siblings then we are more likely to develop affection in our own lives.

Although we may end up being unaffectionate, I strongly believe that this is a learned condition that can be unlearned, or replaced with healthier habits. The key to doing this is to overcome our discomfort and fear of being affectionate. Due to my own upbringing, I became very defensive. If someone were to pat me on the shoulder or attempt to give me a hug, I usually tensed up, giving signals that it was not OK to get close to me. This has been a knee jerk reaction for most of my life. Part of it may be the result of a heightened startle response, a characteristic of post traumatic stress disorder. Regardless of the cause, I have trained myself to be aware and relax when someone shows affection. When people approach and touch my arm or shoulder, I welcome their contact without the fear I once experienced.

In non-threatening situations, I have no trouble being affectionate, and this too was something that I developed as a result of relearning. From my early twenties, I clearly remember a night I went with a friend to a discotheque. My friend and I spotted two attractive women and I asked one of them to dance. With the loud music it was very hard to hear each other and it seemed as though she didn't understand a word I was saying. After dancing, her sister explained to me that she spoke only Polish and that she had just moved to Canada. We ended up going out on a few dates, and although we did not become sexually active, this woman was extremely affectionate in a kind and loving manner. She essentially brought out and developed a part of me that had been hidden and discouraged. Of course, at the time I was quite dysfunctional and didn't pursue the friendship. I still kick myself for that, but the gift she gave me has impacted me tremendously.

I have learned that parents can also learn to become affectionate. Although my family was large, my mother was in many ways isolated. Shortly after meeting the woman from Poland, I began to hug my mother when I finished a visit with her. At first, hugging her was like hugging a cement pillar, but slowly a hand reached out and patted me on the back, which was a major step for her. Within a few weeks she was hugging me, as well as hugging other family members. She later confessed that it was her fear of rejection that kept her from expressing affection and emotion. What a treat it was to watch her, a few months later, greeting my brother Bill with a hug as he walked in the door! These are examples of how affection can be re-introduced into our lives.

What are Emotions?

Emotions - Our Natural Resource

A commonality of being human is our ability to feel and express ourselves through our emotions. How we are feeling tells us a lot about ourselves and what is going on in our lives. Emotions are a common bond among us. Without emotions there is only logic. There would be no loving or caring for one another, nor would there be joy in our achievements. The quest for happiness is a great motivation for all of us. Without emotions, entertainers and musicians would be all out of work. The human race entertains each other by evoking emotions in theatrical plays, musicals, or through the visual effects of a work of art and dance. Revolutions have occurred because of the ability of leaders to stir the emotions of their followers. To a great extent, our emotions add to our lives. Life would be rather boring without the resource of our emotions - a powerful human trait in communication and problem solving.

Unfortunately, most people have never learned to utilize their emotions. In his book *Managing a Difficult or Hostile Audience*, lecturer and organizational troubleshooter Gordon F. Shea writes "Feelings (are) our lost resource. Feelings - good and bad, can be one of our primary tools for problem identification and problem solving." Many of us have lost, or perhaps never developed, the ability to read the feelings of others. Our inherent ability to be tuned into other's feelings has been lost or trained out of us. Since most people have learned to suppress feelings, we also learn to discount the feelings of others. We often listen for just the facts or details of the situation, and we neglect or are unaware of the feelings involved in the situation. Just as sight, smell, touch, hearing, and tasting are important senses, so too are our emotions. While we would not arbitrarily destroy our sight or hearing, many of us have blocked and denied our sense of feeling. Emotions are just as valuable as our other senses.

Instead of seeing emotions as a resource, many of us see our emotions through fearful eyes. We may be afraid that we will be judged as having poor mental health or that we are impulsive and illogical in our decision making. Impulsive and illogical behavior occurs when we are blinded by the strength and intensity of our emotions or if we are emotionally numb and anxious. Emotional intensity can be frightening for many people, however if we process our emotions as we experience them, we are less likely to experience the intensity and anxiety that occurs when our unresolved troubles are triggered by current events.

Even if emotion is present, many people rely solely on intellect and hard numerical data in the process of problem solving. Many successful people from all walks of life often comment on how an appropriate decision was made based on "gut feeling". This gut feeling is part of our emotional side that we often neglect in decision making. How often have you had a feeling or sense about someone or a situation that ended up being correct? As we become more aware of our feelings we can use them as a gauge to measure the impact of others' behavior as well as our own. We can also use our feelings to rate various career choices or to identify needs that are not being met in our lives.

With little understanding of each other's emotions, it is no wonder that there is such a degree of conflict and misunderstanding in the world on international and personal levels. Once I became more in tune with my own emotions, I experienced an increased awareness of others feelings and moods as I became less and less focused on my own troubles. Understanding and listening to the hurt, the sadness, the abandonment, and the fear of others helps establish a basis for understanding and problem solving. The rewards are multiplied when we can share in their joy and happiness!

A Definition of Emotion

Developing an all encompassing definition of emotions is a great challenge and one that may not be met for a number of years. A scientist might wish to measure emotions in terms of physical changes or energy. A medical doctor might wish to measure heart rate and skin temperature, while a psychiatrist might measure chemical levels in the brain. A massage therapist might measure muscle tension, while a yoga teacher would lead one to concentrating on life forces or chakras. Arriving at a definition of emotions is not likely within the scope of any one profession.

What are emotions? What is the essence of the feelings we have? How are they created, released and resolved in our minds? What happens when we do not express them? Do they simply just disappear or are they stored in some other form? Most of the things in this world can be described in terms of color, shape or form, however emotions seem to escape these types of measurements and descriptions. In the following pages you will discover some things that you may already know as well as some new things about emotions. In writing this section, I have tried to convey the concepts of various research and studies. I believe the information is valuable in that we can build a foundation of understanding from which we can learn to accept our emotions.

The study of our emotions and how they manifest themselves in our bodies is far from complete but is definitely evolving. Darwin was one of the first scientists who attempted to explain the emotional processes in humans. Freud added to this field with his pioneering studies in psychiatry. Generally, emotions are thought of as having three distinctive components: a feeling aspect of the emotion; bodily changes such as increased blood pressure, heart beat, as well as hormonal changes; and bodily changes involving the level of muscle tension.

Earlier research has shown that our emotions do evoke physical responses in our bodies. The earliest and most cited study of these responses was done by Ax in 1953. Ax elicited fear in his test subjects by telling them that there was a possibility of a short circuit in his recording apparatus. He then measured face temperature, blood pressure, and galvanic skin response as well as other physical measurements. Ax was able to prove that emotional responses do affect blood pressure and heart rate.

Using only the cardiovascular measurements, the following table was constructed based on Ax's observations:

	Heart Rate	Systolic Blood Pressure	Diastolic Blood Pressure
Fear	+	+	+
Anger	++	+	++
Sadness	-	+	+
Mirth	+	0	0
Sex	0	+	+

Years ago the view advanced by scientists was that the bodily changes were in fact the emotion and that the feelings involved in an emotion were not observable or verifiable. The only way to verify that an emotion was occurring was to ask the person having the emotion. If emotions are to be defined as only bodily changes (such as visceral and skeletal reactions), then artificially produced bodily changes should result in the emotion; however this is not the case. Someone who is artificially stimulated does not experience the tone or feeling. It is now more accepted that the three aspects (feeling, bodily changes and increased muscular tension) need to be present.

In addition, I would argue that a person's values and beliefs at any given time will influence the process of emotional stimulation. A person's belief as to what constitutes a threat or perceived hurt will vary a person's emotional response. Some people are more sensitive than others, resulting in variations in levels of emotional response.

In recent years, new technology has led to a greater understanding of emotions. New scientific advances such as Magnetic Resonance Imaging (MRI) have allowed the medical field to record and review areas of brain activity while emotion is occurring. The identification and description of the emotion is still required from the subject.

In a research paper investigating the emotional experience associated with running and meditation, Jane Harte states that "A well tested, comprehensive, neuro-anatomical map of emotional experience has not yet been found", however our understanding is growing in leaps and bounds.

Central to the understanding of emotion is the study of the Central Nervous System (CNS). Some theories indicate that CNS activity is intrinsic in emotional experience. Studies have shown that emotional behavior releases a substantial number of chemicals and hormones. Other studies regarding the regulation and production of hormones, as well as the secretion process in other glands, have put emphasis on inter-relating central nervous subsystems. Some hormones seem to play an important role in memory, learning and selective attention. Other hormones, such as serotonin, have been linked as well to heightened emotions.

Humans have sometimes been described as walking chemistry sets, but we are also much more than that. Our bodies are much more intelligent than we or science realizes or can presently measure. In a video series on the nature of the mind, Dr. David Suzuki states that "If the doors of perception were cleansed, the world would appear to man as it is.... The door to perception is the brain's own chemicals."

Emotional Energy

Although we may now be able to measure chemical, hormonal, and physical changes in the body as a result of emotions, we still are left with the trouble of defining what the actual feeling of the emotion is. How does it enter my consciousness? How do I resolve it? What process occurs when I grieve or talk things out with a friend? How is my subconscious created in this milieu of chemicals and hormones? Perhaps these answers are still unattainable. Our bodies are very complicated systems. We have yet to understand how ideas are generated by our brain, or how our brain creates our dreams. We are learning about the power of our subconscious mind and its powerful abilities to assist us in problem solving, yet we still do not have an understanding of where our conscious energy comes from.

Most of us would agree that just as emotions can at times drain us, they can also produce vitality and energy in us. In times of joy we feel light, alive and invigorated, while during times of sadness we can feel lethargic. An emotional experience always results in a change in the energy state of the individual experiencing the emotion. Anger or fear tends to raise the energy level of an individual, while one can feel exhausted after a good long cry.

Let's look at the composition of the word "Emotion". Breaking it into two components, we have the letter "E" and the word "motion". In scientific equations, "E" is used to represent energy. The word motion describes an object or entity that is moving and not resting in one place. Our emotions exhibit the same characteristics of energy and motion. The emotion is a form of energy that is not meant to be static. Our emotions are processes through which we move and resolve. We are not meant to be stuck in a particular emotional state. To move from a particular state we must release the energy associated with the emotion.

Perhaps, for the most part, we can use a model of energy to explain our experience of emotions. This emotional energy cannot yet be measured with scientific instruments, but it can be measured in terms of the transfer of the energy into behavior and emotional expression. The one clear facet of emotions is that our emotions generate energy. This energy seems to be created as a reaction to events or circumstances in our lives. If we have been injured then we will feel anger or sadness. If we experience an uplifting moment we can feel joy. The emotions we experience are created and, as we experience these feelings, the energy associated with them is released.

Each emotion we experience and express has a beginning and end to its energy life cycle. Through the expression of emotions we release that energy and become free to move on. The word emotion comes from the word emote, meaning to express.

The experiencing of emotions can have a tremendous effect on our daily lives. Think of a time when we are happy. Our bodies feel active and vibrant. At times when we feel sad or depressed, we tend to feel listless and lethargic. Emotional energy can either add to our daily lives or drain our energy levels. As we release our emotional energy we maintain a sense of balance in our lives. Simply put, emotional energy can either tire us or add zest to our life. If we repress our emotions, we alter and block a vital flow of energy and a process that maintains stability in our mind and body.

If we experience an emotion from beginning to end, the energy of the emotion eventually dissipates. We return to a state of equilibrium. Attempting to block our emotions can drain us of our vitality and ability to experience joy.

Some members of the alternative medicine community have held the belief that unexpressed emotions are stored in muscle tension and that releasing the muscle tension through massage will result in discharge of the emotions. It is evident that emotional expression fully involves many muscle groups.

Frederick Perls, the founder of Gestalt therapy, says that "Emotional excitement mobilized the muscles, the motoric system. Every emotion, then, expresses itself in the muscular system." It is not possible to be angry without muscular tension and movement. Even if we do not express anger, there is an increase in muscular tension as we hold it down. Perls states that "Any disturbance of this excitement metabolism will diminish your vitality". A foundation of Gestalt and other therapies is that the denial and repression of emotions lead to a state of anxiety.

If our emotions are extinguished or denied, particularly through the avoidance of crying, then we must raise the question of what the long term effects of not crying might bring about. Adults may learn whole new repertoires of action or patterns that may serve as substitutes for crying. Often people will use sports, talking or other forms of expression to release their emotional energy.

Emotional Maturity

Achieving emotional health and maturity involves the integration of emotions into our lives. There are two polarities that can indicate a lack of emotional maturity. On one extreme we may run from our emotions. The opposite occurs when we are run by our emotions. Neither of these two states are conducive to emotional health and well-being. What is needed is a sense of balance and the ability to integrate our emotions into our daily lives so that our emotions do not overrun our minds and behavior.

So, how would one define an emotionally mature person? The following words describe the emotionally mature individual:

accepting	expressive	integrated
balanced	constructive	secure
appreciative	self-aware	free

To be emotionally mature means being appropriately expressive, being aware of others, and being secure in one's identity. It also involves having a sound understanding of self and a set of skills or patterns that one uses to deal with everyday challenges as well as other difficulties. Being emotionally mature involves being open minded and having a realistic view of self and others, and knowledge of what one will or will not accept. The emotionally mature person is secure and can be expressive, yet maintain control in emotionally stressful situations.

As a result of these traits, the emotionally mature person can accept that life is difficult, yet derive a satisfaction from life through contributing to the goals and needs of himself and others. Achieving this maturity is a lifelong goal. Increasing our level of maturity begins with accepting that we are emotional and that the expression of emotion in ourselves and others is natural and positive. Living an emotionally mature life allows us to see things as they are, to experience connectedness with others, and to give selflessly to others.

Again, we can look to the Gestalt Therapy views to aid us in our understanding. Frederick Perls writes: "the center of personality is what used to be called the soul: the emotions, the feelings, the spirit. Emotions are not a nuisance to be discharged. The emotions are the most important motors of our behavior."

Recently, in a discussion group on emotions, I posed the question "What do you think of being described as emotional?" The answers surprised me. Common responses were: unbalanced, neurotic, burnt-out, and out of control. I believe these responses reflect a societal discomfort with emotion and people's fears of losing control.

In the Princeton Language Institute's *Synonym and Antonym Finder*, I searched for words that can be used in place of the word "emotional". Some of the words from the list are as follows: ardent, enthusiastic, excitable, feeling, fervent, heartwarming, impassioned, moving, passionate, poignant, responsive, sensitive, sentient, sentimental, spontaneous, tender, touching, warm, and zealous. For words to replace "emotionless", I discovered these adjectives: blank, chill, cold, cool, detached, dispassionate, distant, flat, frigid, icy, impersonal, indifferent, remote, unfeeling, and unimpassioned.

A question we might ask ourselves is "To which group would we like to belong?" The first list describes someone who is living and experiencing relatedness with others. The second list indicates a sense of dissociation and disconnection with others. It is possible to learn to accept our emotions and to begin using emotional words to describe ourselves. Doing so assists us in becoming more emotionally mature.

To become emotionally mature requires changes in our thinking and behavior. We need to learn to be comfortable with the emotional aspect of ourselves and we need to unlearn some of our behaviors. This can be accomplished through a number of ways. Perhaps our healing work, along with support from a counseling group or counselor, will help us gain greater emotional health and maturity

I believe that the training of individuals to block and suppress their emotions leads to a reduced ability to experience joy in our lives. By getting in touch with those suppressed feelings and releasing them, we can restore our emotional health and become happier people. It is important to note that although we may have been trained to avoid expressing emotions, we can unlearn these habits, resolve the emotions, and let the natural healing process occur.

Just as our bodies can heal physically, the human mind can heal emotionally. It is possible to express the emotions and to heal from the hurt or trauma. Just like a physical injury, emotional healing may leave a scar of some sort. But at least we will have healed. We can continue on and begin to feel some of the joys that life has to offer! Our emotions really are a gift.

Depression, fear and sadness can be resolved if we are willing to do the work required. By releasing our pent up emotions we can experience joy, happiness, clearer thinking, and better relationships. We may find some of our health problems lessened due to the extra energy that we will have available to us.

Our eyes may become clearer and our posture may improve, since we will no longer be carrying around the weight of the world on our shoulders. In my own experience, as I became more emotionally connected I found I was receiving feedback that I was becoming more genuine, warm and caring.

With emotional resolution, we will likely find joy a renewed joy in our lives. We will begin to cultivate a relationship with ourselves and begin to discover who we really are without the emotional baggage. We may even discover new interests and hobbies, develop new friendships and end our isolation. We may also begin to remember our past in a clearer more accepting manner. We may begin to forgive ourselves and others and begin living with more serenity, warmth and love in our day to day living. Let go!

Mind, Body and Emotions

Emotions and Physical Health

Time and time again we hear how our physical health is interconnected with our level of stress. How big a role then, does our emotional health play in our physical health? What happens to us if we do not allow ourselves to release and, most importantly, resolve our emotions? What happens to our life expectancy? At various times in my own life, stressful periods have often been followed by times of muscle aches, lethargy, colds, or insomnia. Once the stress was dealt with, these symptoms disappeared. The latest research has shown a great number of links and trends between emotional expression and health.

For starters, hostile and cynical men and women tend to live shorter lives. This is not to say that people who express anger can expect a shorter life, but those who do not resolve their anger and stay hostile have a shorter life expectancy than those who do resolve their anger! Many studies have shown a direct link between unresolved anger and heart disease. If we consider the physical responses that occur when someone is angry, it becomes easy to understand the strain placed on our hearts when subjected to prolonged anger. When we are angry, our blood pressure increases and the heart muscles contract. If we remain angry, our heart is continually under this strain, which can lead to heart disease. Most doctors and nurses recognize that emotions play a large role in patient's blood pressure and heart health.

Links between expressed emotion and glucose control in insulin-dependent diabetes have been identified, as well as a decrease in asthma, after crying. In animals, research has shown an inverse link between coping and tumor susceptibility.

In studies involving the bereaved, widowers showed a decrease in the functioning of the immune system. The immune suppression continued for as much as four months after the initial bereavement, eventually returning to normal with the expression of the grief. The results of the study suggested that those who express their grief are less likely to suffer from disease than those who hide their feelings and loss.

Even smoking can be linked to our emotional state. A recent study has shown that having a cigarette results in certain hormones being released in the brain. These are the same hormones that affect levels of depression. Smokers who cannot quit are more likely to be depressed. Not only does it seem that the nicotine is addictive, but that a smoker who is feeling down will actually get a hormonal lift from having a cigarette! Doctors are now looking at helping these smokers kick the habit by prescribing drugs that help alleviate the depression.

It has also been proposed that difficulties in expressing anger and difficulty controlling intense emotions are factors that can pre-dispose oneself to depression and chronic pain. In an article summary for the Journal of Consulting and Clinical Psychology, the authors state that "Chronic pain and depression may be disturbances or failures to process intensely emotional information, with concomitant disturbances both in the body's immune system and in interpersonal relationships."

It seems that suppressing emotions does affect our physical health. Using energy to suppress our emotions results in a drain of the resources we normally use to fight colds and other health problems. We will be more susceptible to stress and fatigue. This explains the fact that when we are under stress, we often tend to get sick. Resolving emotional issues often brings about the reduction of health problems.

Allergies have been attributed to unresolved grief and the allergy symptoms have disappeared upon the release and resolution of the emotions. In my own case, allergy symptoms all but disappeared after the resolution of my emotional issues. I now consider myself to be allergy free and enjoy the company of a wonderful cat!

Others have experienced changes in their body cycles once they began to face and express their bottled emotions. A close friend of mine began having regular menstrual periods after beginning to get in touch with, releasing, and resolving her emotional issues.

In reviewing *Mind/Body Health* by Hafen, Karren, Frandsen and Smith, it is clear that there is a correlation between one's emotional state and accidents, allergies and asthma, arthritis, back pain and cancer, dental cavities, diabetes, hypertension, insomnia, irritable bowel syndrome and many other syndromes and maladies. However, telling someone with a disease that emotions play a big role in their disease does not help them cope with their disease, nor does it help them get better or help them deal with their emotions. It is important to note that a correlation indicates only that one variable changes as the other variable changes. I remember reading in my statistics course of a study that showed a correlation between the stork population of Greenland and the North American birth rate! Although two variables may show a correlation, it can not be assumed that the presence of one variable is the cause of the change in the other variable. Other factors or causes may be at work.

When discussing emotions and health issues we want to take care in realistically identifying the true causes of illness. Recently we have become more aware of the role that our psychological state plays in our health. We have learned through the work of Jonas Salk in the 1960's that illness is based on genetic, behavioral, nervous and immune system relationships. Instead of looking at the causes of diseases as a simplistic model, we can now understand that they can have a number of interrelated causes. We therefore would want to be careful and state that unresolved emotions are not necessarily the sole cause of the allergies, asthma, illness, or health problems. If a person has allergic tendencies, then the addition of emotional stress is likely to bring on a stronger allergic reaction or an attack of asthma. By dealing with the emotional component we can reduce some of the factors contributing to the illness.

The Healing Brain

One of the most interesting books I have come across is *The Healing Brain, a Scientific Reader*. This collection of articles regarding the brain contains a chapter titled *The Brain as a Health Maintenance Organization*. Authors Robert Ornstein and David S. Sobel write "We need to recognize that the brain is not primarily for educating, not for speaking and thinking, but it is more like a gland, part of the body and a system to the mind and body."

Our brain works to maintain stability in countless subsystems. It controls the beating of our hearts, blood pressure, the expansion and contraction of our lungs to provide ourselves with needed oxygen, the transfer of oxygen into our blood stream. Our brain also controls an internal pharmaceutical system, maintaining thousands of chemicals in our bodies. It keeps us from danger, holds us close to friends and family. It creates dreams for us, many of which can be analyzed to solve problems, and guides us through various life crises.

The brain, however, spends a minimal amount of time on conscious functions such as preparing for communication, processing music, organizing, writing or preparing for other human activities. The brain spends most of its time maintaining homeostasis in a changing environment. The body and brain must continually adapt to change. As individuals, we are always growing emotionally, spiritually and in knowledge, and the brain must adapt and deal with these changes. The brain therefore, is attempting to maintain stability during an ongoing process of change.

To understand the brain we need to recognize that the brain can be considered as one large gland, which under various influences, attempts to return to a state of equilibrium. If we experience an event that triggers an emotional response, the brain will attempt to return to a state of equilibrium through a number of actions. These actions include the release of emotional energy through crying, laughing, trembling, blushing, increased muscle tension, or a host of other forms of energy release.

The brain consists of numerous subsystems that manage this change. Science is just beginning to obtain a grasp of the complexity and inner workings of these systems. Obviously, with the new discoveries we are making about the brain and its resistance to disease, we are at the beginning of a new era of medicine and healing. We are also more aware of the role that hope plays in the health of an individual. Ornstein and Sobel also write that "recent discoveries about endorphin, immune and cardiovascular systems, combined with new studies of brain physiology, human evolution and cognitive psychology point to a new understanding of this most mysterious organ...."

Besides being an organ that regulates and maintains our bodies, the brain is a fantastic agent of healing. It restores us to health after an injury. Almost magically, our body will heal from a cut or an infection. It protects us when the injury is severe by shutting down some systems. It is a healing brain. But the healing work that the brain does is not limited to physical injury alone. When we allow ourselves to grieve a loss our brain allows us to heal from the loss. When we proceed through the emotional process of letting go, we return to a state of stability.

Ornstein and Sobel conclude that "Healing does not merely restore the mind or body to its condition before the illness, but more usually it brings about a lasting change." It is a fact that even the most primitive organisms possess the ability to self-heal. While much attention has been focused on medical cures and medications, it may also be reasonable to focus more on our capacity to heal that exists at every level of evolution. This ability to heal is present in all living things. Although healing can be considered to be the process of repairing physical or emotional damage, there is often a greater aspect to the repairing process. Healing brings about a permanent change in the person or organism that allows us to cope with new situations. Focusing on the mind and body's natural ability to heal in the next stages of research is certainly warranted. As Nietzsche states "that which does not kill me makes me stronger".

A new field that studies how the body and mind interact in healing is psycho-neuroimmunology. This field is beginning to understand the relationships between neurons, synapses, neuropeptides, and cells that form that form the body's communication network. This field of study is learning that the brain, glands and immune system are joined and interlinked with one another. It is a bi-directional network of communication. It is now known that neurons communicate with one another through neuropeptides. The neuropeptides can produce effects in regions of the body that are different and far away from the location of the neuron that produced the neuro-peptide.

We are beginning to learn that emotions do not just occur in the brain, but are linked to the whole body. This explains or correlates with the idea of a "gut feeling", that our emotional state is often reflected in our eyes, or that an emotional experience may trigger a shortness of breath. Many fields of holistic medicine focus on the whole body and mind when treating various illnesses. A sense of the body as a whole is beginning to develop in the research into healing and immunology. Instead of focusing on the area of injury, the body, mind and person must be treated as a whole. This form of treatment has been the basis of treatments such as acupuncture, massage and various other forms of healing.

Until recently, the idea that emotions can build up has never been proven by science. We are learning that emotional trauma has significant effects on the body's chemistry and that emotional expression brings about change in the body and mind state. The latest scientific research has identified a number of communication systems in the body that tend to support the notion of emotions occurring as a whole body experience. In *The Body Keeps Score: Memory and the Evolving Psychobiology of Post traumatic Stress*, Bessel A. Van der Kolk M.D. describes some of the effects of trauma on the chemical and hormone levels in the body. It is now understood that emotional trauma brings about long lasting changes in body chemistry. I believe that one day scientists will prove that emotions are in fact stored in the body through changes in energy, chemical balance and muscle tone.

In a discussion of holistic medicine, Dr. Leo Roy stated that "An emotional trauma can do more damage to the liver than six months of drinking." Our emotional traumas and hurts can be felt throughout the whole body. Muscle tension, a knotting in the stomach, back aches, high blood pressure, and sugar levels are all affected by our emotional state. Should we suppress or avoid our emotions, we end up placing pressure on our body to cope with an emotional imbalance. Expression and resolution will assist our returning to a more balanced state. Perhaps the intrusive flashbacks, somatic symptoms, dreams and emotional distresses are clues that the mind presents to us to alert us to our need to do some healing work.

Mark Linden O'Meara

The Benefits of Expression

Having looked at adverse effects of emotional stress on our health, let's begin to look at the positive outcomes of letting our emotions take their natural course. As mentioned earlier, tears are a natural response to a loss or emotional injury as well as the gift of joy. A great number of chemicals and hormones are released through our tears when we cry. In *It's Never Too Late to Have a Happy Childhood*, author Claudia Black writes "Where there is loss there are tears; tears are the elixir of recovery."

Laughter

In creating a therapeutic group climate for elders, studies have shown that laughter is one of the top ten components. It is not possible to be depressed when we are laughing. Laughter brings about chemical changes in our body that help us fight illness and disease. One of the classic tales of curing illness by laughter is told in Norman Cousins' book *Anatomy of an Illness*. Cousins had been diagnosed with a fatal illness. He cured himself by booking himself into a hotel room, sending out for Marx Brothers movies, and watching segments of Candid Camera. Cousins' pain diminished and as he says "The more I laughed, the better I got."

Laughter has been credited with restoring balance in the body, returning blood pressure to normal, bringing about relaxation, and improving circulation. Studies also link improved respiration and heart rates to the benefits of laughter. An article called "Laughter and Health" published as early as 1928, the doctor described "laboratory evidence which established that a hearty, throaty laugh momentarily compensates for either high or low blood pressure."

In another study, two groups of college students were fed the same diet. One group of students was treated to lectures by a professional comedian, while the other group was treated to scientific lectures. Not surprisingly, the results of the test showed that the students who experienced the comedy routine at lunch time were healthier, with a noticeable improvement in digestion.

Finally, the journal abstract for *Laughter: Nature's Epileptoid Catharsis*, by Gerard Grumet, states that the article "depicts laughter as a symbolic triggered release mechanism that unleashes instinctive drive energies associated with survival and lowers anxiety in the process."

The Healing Power of Tears

Shakespeare understood the power of tears when he wrote "To weep is to make less the depth of grief." In recent years, scientists have been proving that tears are beneficial to our health and well being. My own personal experience has proven this time and time again. Scientists have known for over 35 years that emotional tears vary from tears produced as a result of peeling an onion. Tears released on account of emotions contain more protein as well as one of the body's most powerful pain killers - beta-endorphin.

Dr. William Frey of the Dry Eye and Tear Research Center states that people who cry "may be removing, in their tears, chemicals that build up during emotional stress." Dr. Alan Wolfelt of the University of Colorado Medical School states that "In my clinical experience with thousands of mourners, I have observed physical changes following the expression of tears....Not only do people feel better after crying; they also look better." In *The Brain as a Health Maintenance Organization*, authors Robert Ornstein and David S. Sobel respond to the question of why people cry. The authors state that recent evidence implies that crying "may be a way in which the body disposes of toxic substances". Many people believe that crying helps them to reduce tension. In the long run, a good cry makes them feel better.

Researchers at the State University of New York at Buffalo have also found that crying is common among emotionally healthy adults and that crying is not necessarily a symptom of depression. In a study of people in their late sixties, researchers found that the adults had a good cry every two or three weeks. The main reasons for crying were simply to reduce feelings of stress. In a study by the University of Pittsburgh, it was documented that there is a definite correlation between stress-related illness and a reluctance to cry. Scientists are now learning that crying seems to reduce our stress levels and increase our level of health

Tears have also been known to bring about changes in the behavior of people, even children, with seemingly disturbed behavior patterns. An article in the *International Review of Psycho-Analysis* describes how a child, completely withdrawn and with a destructive behavior pattern, broke out into a weeping fit in one of her therapy sessions. These weeping fits, which contained feelings of rage, despair and sorrow, continued for a number of sessions during which a change in the character of her appearance as well as in her behavior began. The article suggests that the release of tears was the first phase of her psychotherapy.

Other benefits of tears have been identified as well. In addition to reducing asthma attacks, studies have indicated that crying seems to reduce the occurrence of hives. After crying in therapy sessions, patients have lower blood pressure, lower body temperatures, and more synchronized brain wave patterns, as well as notable psychological improvements. In fact, the benefits of crying have been scientifically known for almost a century. A study by Borquist in 1906 reported that 54 out of 57 respondents believed that crying had positive results. A study by Weiner found that asthma attacks, which were for a long time thought to be psychosomatic, ceased as a result of crying.

The belief that crying has positive effects was developed over two thousand years ago. Aristotle believed that crying could cleanse the mind through a process of catharsis. Catharsis is a means of reducing emotional stress through the expression of emotion. Many others have echoed Aristotle's thoughts. Suggestions regarding the benefits of catharsis can be found in native literature and the writings of Freud. Aristotle believed that theater and drama serve a useful purpose in catharsis. Sobel and Ornstein write "Many people attend movies and plays that they know beforehand are, shall we say, elicitors of psychogenic lacrimation, or tearjerkers". People may often feel comfortable crying during a movie and not experience any embarrassment or regret, knowing that the tears bring benefits.

Although we know that chemicals are present in the emotional tears, we do not know what function the release of these chemicals serve. Some of the chemicals such as beta-endorphin, are responsible for relieving pain. Other evidence has become known to indicate that tears play a greater role than we had previously considered. In the literal sense, crying and sobbing may actually be cleansing the mind, thus validating the original theory of catharsis. Perhaps tears and crying are the body's mechanism for releasing emotional tension and for restoring the body to a state of equilibrium.

In addition to the release of tears, crying results in a number of physiological processes. Although a person in the stages of grief may show less facial expression and muscle tone, facial tension actually is increased. In a study of facial expression and tension, it was noted that facial tension increases in the forehead which pulls the eyebrows together. Increased tension can also be found in the jaw and mouth, which results in a pulling down of the corners of the mouth. Our body releases a great deal of muscular tension when we cry. Sobbing with tears will cause a reflex that reduces and resolves the muscle tension associated with grief. Emotional release, often referred to as catharsis, will lead to a reduction in tension and that previously observed effects virtually disappear.

Researchers are now focusing on contents of emotional tears and attempting to identify the content and purpose of these chemicals. With this new knowledge, it is certainly reasonable to conclude that emotional tears play a very important role and function in the emotional and physical health of the individual.

While crying may be a natural response to a hurt, to many of us it does not feel natural at all. Not all of us have been taught to feel comfortable with crying. In our childhood we may have been punished for crying rather than being rewarded. Most of us are unaware of the healing power of tears. Crying is the main action that helps us to release our suppressed emotions and heal. Although we may not be comfortable or admit to crying, it is a natural response to hurt. The normal and natural response to hurt is to cry, thus releasing our pain. To control or block our tears is to deny our body's natural method of releasing and healing. Although we know that our tears release chemicals, no one knows what happens to those chemicals if we do not cry. We now know that crying is necessary for emotional healing. During my own process of catharsis and healing, I kept thinking that the tears I was releasing were somehow cleansing my body of the stresses that I had accumulated.

Many of us, however, are afraid of our tears. We may fear that if we start to cry, we will be unable to stop. I too felt a fear of losing control, however I reminded myself that for years I had exercised the discipline of keeping things under control and that I still had those skills. I also found that as the wave of emotion was approaching, it seemed much larger compared to the view I had of its size once it had passed! To give myself the courage to face it, I constantly reminded myself of the benefits that expression would bring.

Most of us need to re-learn that crying brings about healing. Fearful of tears, I began to learn and trust that crying actually soothes and brings about a reduction in stress. I discovered that if I was willing to let go and express my emotions, then the stressful energy contained in them would dissipate and pass. The more I expressed my emotions the less each day's events were clouded by past events that I had not resolved.

Crying is a natural process by which we can release the energy in our emotions. It restores our mind and body to a more natural balance. When we suppress our tears we end up using a great deal of energy to hold down or keep that energy at bay. We may feel as though we have stopped the tears, but what we have really done is pushed the tears and hurt into our subconscious. The feelings are not dealt with and the suppression ends up blocking our ability to feel joy and companionship.

With the release of chemicals through our tears, our body heals emotionally and we become more emotionally healthy. Once we have resolved our emotional tension we tend to be less isolated, since we no longer need to keep others at a distance fearing that we will break down emotionally. We are able to tolerate discharge in others and we are able to express ourselves more openly and to listen to others without the fear of old injuries being re-stimulated.

There are still many things to be learned about the various

balances that occur in our body. It is certain though, that suppressing our emotions stops the natural process of our body. Repressing our emotions can lead to isolation, a reduction of clarity of thought, and reduced tolerance for emotions in others. Grief, for one, is a very isolating emotion. Fortunately, these symptoms are not permanent and we can restore ourselves from these symptoms through emotional expression and the healing power of tears.

Mark Linden O'Meara

CRY (IF YOU WANT TO)

Cry if you want to I won't tell you not to
I won't try to cheer you up I'll just be here if you want me
It's no use in keeping a stiff upper lip
You can weep you can sleep you can loosen your grip
You can frown you can drown, and go down with the ship
You can cry if you want to

Don't even apologize for venting your pain
It's something that to me you don't need to explain
I don't need to know why, I don't think it's insane
You can cry if you want to

The windows are closed, the neighbors aren't home
If it's better with me than to do it alone
I can draw all the curtains and unplug the phone
You can cry if you want to

You can stare at the ceiling and tear at your hair
You can swallow your feelings and swagger and swear
You can throw things and show things and I wouldn't care
You can cry if you want to

I won't make fun of you I won't tell anyone
I won't analyze what you do or you should've done
I won't advise you to go and have fun
You can cry if you want to.

I can't make it all go away
I don't have any answers I've nothing to say
But I'm not going to lie to you and say it's okay
You can cry if you want to

Cry if you want to I won't tell you not to
I won't try to cheer you up
I'll just be here if you want me to be near you
Maybe I'll cry too

Emotions and Our Soul

Self Esteem

As mentioned early, babies seem to have an unrepressed ability to express emotions and discharge. Depending on our upbringing or due to events in our lives, we may have developed a conditioned response of ignoring our emotions and trying to avoid the pain in our lives.

In his book *The Six Pillars of Self Esteem*, Nathaniel Brandon says that to deny one's emotions usually results in a loss of self-esteem. This occurs whether we are children or adults. Denying our emotions causes us to lose contact with our inner self and our ability to care for our soul. It is our soul that makes us human and we are most human when we find a deep connection with our soul.

In *Care of the Soul*, Thomas Moore writes that "Soul is not a thing, but a quality or a dimension of experiencing life and ourselves". Our soul can be defined as that which holds our values, beliefs, and center of being. In caring for our soul we must know how our soul expresses itself and we must be able to observe and be connected with it. Moore states that "We cannot care for the soul unless we are familiar with its ways." To be familiar with our soul involves fully experiencing life and observing our reactions to it.

Life is a process of encounters which are often viewed as either positive or negative. Often we try to avoid the negative issues and feelings in our lives, but in doing so, we miss valuable lessons to be learned. Moore states: "When people observe the ways in which the soul is manifesting itself, they are enriched rather than impoverished." To listen to our soul, especially in times of trouble, brings great rewards. Facing the part of us that we fear the most is often what we must do to free ourselves of pain and sadness. Being open to the pain of the soul brings awareness of ourselves and solutions to our problems. Solving those problems brings about an internal strength that we can carry forward with us. As Moore writes "When you regard the soul with an open mind, you begin to find the messages that lie within the illness, the corrections that can be found in remorse and other uncomfortable feelings, and the necessary changes requested by depression and anxiety."

It truly is a myth that we can control our thoughts and feelings. For a long time I believed that I could control my feelings and the price I paid was high. There are certain behaviors and things we can do for ourselves to improve our emotional state, but this is different from accepting the thoughts and feelings that come into our consciousness. By attempting to selectively control our thoughts and emotions we block access to our soul. We need to let our soul be free to express itself. What we can control is our behavior around these emotions and thoughts.

Currently there are many techniques and seminars aimed at providing a quick fix for emotional problems. While some of these techniques seem to provide a reprieve, many are not long lasting, as the original problem has not been dealt with. Some of these techniques can be helpful though in pulling ourselves through a difficult time. In *The Power of Positive Thinking*, Norman Vincent Peale states that "It is important to discover why you have these feelings... That requires analysis and will take time. We must approach the maladies of our emotional life as a physician probes to find something wrong physically. This cannot be done immediately."

Peale importantly states "An excellent and normal release from heartache is to give way to grief". In many cultures, the expression and showing of grief is considered to be embarrassing and is discouraged. It may be considered foolish to express oneself through the expression of tears or sobbing. This, however, is a violation of one of our natural mechanisms for the release of emotional tension and pain. As Peale says, "This is a denial of the law of nature. It is natural to cry when pain or sorrow comes. It is a relief mechanism provided in the body by Almighty God and should be used." To restrain emotion, to suppress it, or to inhibit it is to rob ourselves of our natural means for eliminating the pressure of life. To deny our emotions is similar to denying that we must eat and drink to nourish ourselves. As with other needs, we must not indulge in them, but we must not deny them altogether. Peale states that "a good cry by either man or woman is a release from heartache."

The Nature of Depression

Everyone gets depressed at some time or another. It is a fact of life. Although often labeled as an illness, depression can be a normal reaction to various events that occur in our lives. Depression is something that hits almost all of us at one time or another. Depression can occur as a result of a loss, a success, achieving a goal, a physical injury, a personal trauma, or simply as a result of a build up of daily events. Just as there are many types of losses, there are many causes for depression. It is important to stress the fact that depression is a natural response to these occurrences and it is normally a transient mental state that will be resolved.

In surveying the discussion groups on the Internet, I found that one of the busiest newsgroups was the support group for depression. In this newsgroup people exchanged information on medication, side effects, signs of depression, and things that facilitated the resolution of a depression. Many provided encouragement for others, and for some it was a chance to express themselves. The number of postings to this group gives an indication of the number of people who are affected at one time or another by depression. These individuals report lowered spirits, a loss of self-esteem, difficulty sleeping, and a difference in perspective. Other symptoms may include a loss of energy, weight loss, changes in appetite, and physical complaint, without any medical basis.

Generally speaking, there are two types of depression that the fields of psychiatry and psychology try to treat. The first type is called an organic depression that usually is the result of an imbalance of chemicals in the brain. This type of depression usually responds well to treatment by medication. The second type of depression is called a reactive or situational depression that is usually a result of unresolved life experiences or an emotional trauma.

Some of us may have an organic depression that can be treated with medication, while some of us may have a non-organic or situational depression caused by personal traumas or losses as described above. In some cases it may be a combination of organic and non-organic depression. Medication can help resolve an organic depression, while counseling and therapy can help to resolve a non-organic depression.

Depression can result from a great number of factors. Change of any type, be it geographical location, lifestyle, daily routine or contact with others can be a contributing factor in depression. Any change that involves someone or something of value can be a catalyst for depression. The process of life in itself often involves re-evaluating our beliefs and values. A process of developing these values may seem like a depression. A process of transition, such as a job change, or even achieving adulthood can bring about depression. Any process of change (such as growing up) involves change and transition. Each transition or change involves letting go of something and accepting something new. In *The Secret Strength of Depression*, Dr. Frederich Flach writes "in order to move successfully from one phase to the next, a person must be able to experience depression in a direct and meaningful way."

Depression often results when we discover that our life does not measure up to what we would like it to be. As in my case, unresolved grief can also lead to depression. The same holds true of beliefs we hold about ourselves that keep limiting our self esteem. Depression can also be caused by poor thinking patterns as well. Often a feeling of sadness or hurt will be created by our personal belief systems, which may add to feelings of hurt from the past. Depression may also result from a lack of direction in life, or a lack of short term goals.

One of the drawbacks to our current description of depression is that many professionals do not differentiate between depression and ongoing sadness. The term depression is a wide, sweeping term used to describe a condition that has numerous causes. Long-term depression can be the result of problems in a person's thinking and attitudes, while unresolved issues and trauma can prolong sadness resulting from the event. People who have avoided feelings or who are suffering from a significant loss may be characterized as depressed, yet it is grieving work that the individual may need to complete to resolve the sadness. In some cases, the events may be difficult to identify because the person has avoided their feelings and has not become appropriately and sufficiently upset by the events. A chronic feeling of sadness may also be indicative of the fact that certain areas of a person's life need changing. Some people may have difficulties relating to others, or an unsatisfying job. Without resolution or positive change, the sadness will be an ongoing component of their lives. In the cases of earlier abuse, the depression may be the result of a wound to the individual's character or soul which requires a process of grieving, self-acceptance and healing to resolve the depression.

From the above, we can conclude that the causes of depression are numerous. As well, there are some generalities about depression that should be examined. Depression has sometimes been described as anger turned inwards, but it is not fair to say that all depressions are the result of unexpressed anger. In recent years, research has also led us to believe that depression is an illness resulting from chemical deficiencies in the brain. What remains to be seen, however, is whether these deficiencies are the cause of the depression or a symptom of the depression. In labeling the depression as a disease, some may feel powerless to resolve the depression, while in fact, they might be able to learn some behaviors that will naturally raise chemical levels in the brain. This area of research is so new that the effect on the brain of "healthy pleasures" such as singing, meditation, yoga, and physical exercise are not yet understood or measured.

Although a time of depression is not an easy period for anyone, it can be a time of tremendous change and growth. As Dr. Flach writes,"to experience acute depression is an opportunity for a person not just to learn more about himself, but to become more whole than he was. Not only does depression afford a chance for insight, but 'falling apart' can accelerate the process of reordering one's life after a serious stress."

Although depression reduces vitality and makes it difficult to find solutions to problems, there are benefits to depression. Often, creative people will attribute the creation of their work to an episode of depression. Many individuals who have made significant life changes also attribute the changes they made to periods of depression. Often these people will emerge from a depression with a new and exciting view of life. Similar to the idea of the phoenix that crashes into the fire yet emerges as a beautiful new bird, a depression that is experienced and resolved allows us to rebound to new levels of understanding and meaning. Dr. Flach writes that "to be creative in any sense, a person must be able to relinquish old and fixed assumptions that block a fresh appraisal of a situation." Perhaps to be creative also involves being open to the experience of moving through a depression.

Perhaps as a society we need to challenge our view of mental health. Society has generally viewed the happy-go-lucky person as the well adjusted person. Now we are understanding that episodes of depression are a natural part of life and of growth. Perhaps the person who gets angry, cries, laughs or gets embarrassed, and who works through a depression, is the well adjusted person. In an Internet posting on the topic of depression, an individual posed the question "When will I be normal again?" Perhaps a better line of reasoning might be "I am depressed. I am normal. How long will this last?."

Relationships and Emotional Baggage

Relationships in themselves are processes of learning about one another. All relationships require effort and communication to resolve issues that arise. If one person in the relationship is much more aware of their emotions than the other, then an imbalance occurs in the relationship. All is not lost however, since if one is willing to discover and express one's feelings then both can grow in their understanding of each other.

A genuine relationship is difficult if one or both partners in the relationship are unable to be genuine with themselves. Someone who seeks a genuine relationship will likely have trouble attracting or connecting with another genuine person simply because of the walls they have built up around their own emotions. These walls may have been erected long ago as a defense mechanism. The walls are still being maintained even though they no longer serve the person. The problem lies in the fact that the individual may not know how to tear down the walls.

Suppressing our emotions usually harms our relationships in the long run. When we suppress, we do not communicate with the other person nor do we resolve issues. These unresolved issues end up making us more sensitive and cloud the real issues in a relationship. Many of us have been raised to believe that blocking or ignoring a feeling or problem may cause it to go away. We may think we have dealt with the issue but in reality it has just been pushed below the surface. This may hinder our communication in the future.

Blocking our emotions is not a true solution for us. In the long run, we end up having day to day issues that trigger the emotions that we think we have dealt with. Unresolved and unexpressed emotions are like an unhealed wound. Until we take the time to let the wound heal, any attempts to use the injured part will only bring back the pain of the old wound or injury.

When we bottle up our emotions we may end up compromising our relationship with ourselves and others. We may become depressed and communication with others may become difficult as it filters through the walls we have built up around our emotions. We may end up giving the impression that we want to be left alone even though it's the exact opposite that we want.

Regardless of the type of numbing mechanism we use (consciously or unconsciously), it usually takes a great deal of energy to suppress or avoid our emotions. Although we do not have a method of measuring that energy, we can see the effect in our lives. We may not wake up refreshed in the morning. We may be listless and tire easily. We may also have less concentration and poorer memory skills. If we are the type that has stayed extremely busy, we may be afraid to slow down for fear of what we might feel or find.

Often the intense emotions we feel towards someone may be the result of underlying emotions that we may not be aware of. In most relationships we experience day to day events that cause emotional responses. Our response, however, will be greatly determined by the deeper and more subtle feelings we have for that person. If on a deeper level we are angry with someone, then our response to an event will more likely be anger. If we are passive, then this behavior only adds to the underlying tone of anger.

Because we have suppressed our emotions we have probably built emotional walls around ourselves that keep us isolated from others and keep us from feeling and connecting with others. Any backlog of emotions can be a hindrance to a relationship, whereas emotional expression between two people who are comfortable with their own emotions will lead to a greater bond between partners. Perhaps it is time to make better use of our energy, to open up to others and let them help us and to begin the healing process.

Emotional Avoidance

The Masks We Wear

One of the techniques that so many of us use to maintain a degree of emotional safety is to wear an emotional mask. We end up becoming skilled actors or actresses in maintaining a front to others. Often people are seen as happy-go-lucky, yet they are hurting inside and too afraid to let others know what they are really thinking and feeling. In my childhood I became very skilled at hiding my hurt from others. It was a defense mechanism that saved me from additional shame and ridicule and that I carried into my adult life. In most cases, it is not because people wish to deceive anyone that they wear these masks, but simply because it is the best coping mechanism they have learned. As well, an emotional mask may also serve as a form of denial until the person is ready to face the issues that have brought about the emotional pain.

At times our masks are necessary to protect ourselves and they may have been an appropriate defense at some time. As adults, these masks may no longer be effective tools for daily living and may now be harming or detracting from our enjoyment of life and sharing with others. To open up to another requires trust and courage, especially if we have been emotionally abused by others who were in a position of authority or trust. To become an emotionally healthy person involves identifying our masks and beginning to come out from behind the mask with ourselves and those we trust. Peeking out from behind the mask allows others to see ourselves in a more open manner. The more we work at removing the mask, the more genuine we become. We are then able to form deeper connections with ourselves and others. Which of the following masks do you use and which do you recognize as others' masks?

The Smiler

The smiler is a person who always seems to greet us with a happy face. They seem to be consistently up when we greet them, but their smile really masks their true feelings. When with closer friends the smiler may let down their guard and confide some of their true feelings, but with the appearance of an outsider, the mask will usually quickly reappear. While able to trust close friends, the smiler will maintain a front among most people. If asked how they are truly feeling, they might begin to honestly tell you, but would not likely be willing to face any pain they are feeling.

Polyanna-ism or Pronoid

Polyanna-ism refers to people who always seem extremely happy. They go around saying how wonderful all the rain is! Sometimes their excessively positive attitudes will begin to bother others. They never seem to get depressed and nothing seems to bother them. They may try to force their happiness onto others. In truth, they may be hurting deeply yet cannot show this side of themselves to others. Their behavior serves as a form of denial of the real pain that they cannot yet face.

Truly, it would be wonderful if one could maintain a life that would generate such a state of happiness, but life has its "ups and downs" and therefore most people have ups and downs too. Life contains many issues that need to be worked on and resolved. Someone who is always up is not likely connected with their own feelings and issues, and is probably in a state of denial. The important question is whether their joy is genuine or a mask. Does this type of person have the ability to express and experience the wide range of emotions, or are they denying a side of their emotional spectrum and self?

As a form of denial, the pronoid will often mask pain by focusing on others. The pronoid will act in a manner that gives an impression of great concern for friends and co-workers. At times, however, when challenged emotionally, this mask of concern will show its cracks.

As an opposite of the paranoid, the pronoid often lives in a fantasy in which they overvalue themselves and overestimate their control of events in their lives. They may make statements about controlling their own destiny, and will attribute circumstantial occurrences to their well-developed sense of willpower.

In an article in the *Medical Ethics Journal*, psychologist

Richard P. Benthal argues that the happiness syndrome is a mood disturbance. Dr. Benthal suggests that the pronoid is really out of touch with reality. The pronoid lives a tinted view in which, as Dr. Benthal states, "mere acquaintances are seen as close friends. Politeness and pleasantries are interpreted as deep friendships." The pronoid has difficulty expressing their true feelings about others and may be masking anger as well.

The Neutral/Flat Mask

An emotionally neutral person is someone who never seems to express any emotions at all. Their facial expression will remain mostly flat, with little smiling or expression of joy in their eyes. It is difficult to tell whether the emotionally neutral or flat person is up or down or anywhere in between, and rarely, if ever, does the neutral mask allow anger to be shown.

They have become very good at masking their emotions even if it is no longer intentional. This mask makes it difficult for them to experience closeness with others.

The Defensive Mask

Defensiveness is something we often display when our beliefs or behavior is challenged. In some cases, we may even become defensive when someone tries to help us. While it usually results in frustration for the other party, a defensive mask serves the purpose of protecting us from hurt. The defensive person keeps others at a safe distance, thus preventing emotions and pain from surfacing. Often considered a form of denial, defensiveness is a way of communicating that the mask wearer is not ready to deal with the pain. To remove the mask requires a degree of trust and willingness to face some pain. Defensiveness often means "I don't want to get hurt".

The Victim Mask

The person wearing the victim mask is someone who often talks about his or her problems but does not achieve resolution of the emotional content. The victim may often seem sad most of the time and look and feel as though they are carrying the weight of the world on their shoulders. They try to have a good time but there always seems to be something dragging them down.

They may demonstrate all the symptoms of depression, but be unwilling to admit that they are hurting or know why they feel down most of the time. They work hard at trying to feel happy but with all of the best intentions, they just do not seem to succeed at achieving much joy in their lives. Time and time again, their state seems to drop down into depression.

The victim will often blame others for misfortunes without truly looking at their emotional side and seeking to admit the depth of their emotion. Often the solution to the victim mask is to develop awareness of family roles, set boundaries and to realize that they have choices other than suffering or being a scapegoat.

The Busy Mask

One of the common techniques used to avoid feeling is keeping extremely busy. The busy mask wearers take on extra work and volunteer for causes that take up a great deal of time. They do not know how to relax and have difficulty slowing down from a hectic schedule that many people would have trouble keeping up with. Each of their evenings are usually booked and to get time with them may mean booking it a few weeks ahead.

Although they give the impression that they really enjoy what they are doing, and perhaps they do, the busy mask is really a defense from facing themselves and their emotions. They are so busy that they do not afford themselves the time to be with themselves. They also likely fear time in which they have nothing to do. It can be next to impossible to relax with a busy type as they will find some extra task to do.

The trap that the busy mask generates is that the person may burnout over time and may be forced to slow down. The busy mask usually results in a catch-22 situation where it is painful to keep so busy, but slowing down also means facing emotional pain. The person wearing the busy mask will need to slow down gradually, because to slow down abruptly can be a tremendous shock. As with all illnesses and problems, prevention is the best cure!

The Intellectual/Rationalization Mask

A very important idea to consider is that emotions are not logical and that it is impossible to focus on thinking and on our emotions at the same time. By keeping all of our thoughts on an intellectual basis we can effectively avoid our emotional side and keep the emotions at bay. The cost of staying in our intellectual side is that our relationships suffer due to a lack of emotional content and connection. A person wearing the intellectual mask will be able to discuss ideas and ideas at length, but will have difficulty sharing feelings and at times may be intense in their discussion of ideas.

The intellectual mask may also be manifested in a rationalization of events. By thinking rather than feeling, the intellectual will rationalize events and behavior to the point that their feelings are dismissed. In both cases, however, the removal or dropping of the mask will bring back the associated feelings.

The Fatigue Mask

Being tired most of the time can be the result of stress or a medical condition, but it can also be a method of avoiding life's issues. By staying in bed or by avoiding participation we can also avoid dealing with the issues of the day. Chronic sleeping in can often be a sign of emotional tension.

The person with the fatigue mask can often drop the mask if some event truly interests them. Once that event passes they will likely revert to old habits of avoiding social activities in favor of what they may call rest. In fact, the sleeping in late does not usually result in a feeling of being more rested but simply perpetuates a feeling of listlessness and little accomplishment.

With the fatigue mask, one can shorten the number of active hours, which in turn reduces the number of hours that the individual is in contact with the subtleties of their pain.

The Joker/Clown Mask

Many of us have been around someone who knew all the latest jokes and could come up with a funny or witty line at a moment's notice. These people can be fun to have around but this behavior turns into a mask when the person uses the jokes to keep people at a distance or to hide their pain. Especially with jokes, it is important to be appropriate. Can the person tell a joke but also share something personal with you?

It is often much easier to be flippant than to show a deeper understanding and caring attitude. Humor is often used as a way of masking serious issues. In addition, the joker or clown so often pulls jokes that when they actually open up or discloses something, the disclosure may be taken for granted or discounted. This occurs simply because people are expecting a punch line.

Often ,to lose the joker mask we need to convince others of our serious side. It may involve some personal publicity work in trying to change others' image of ourselves. The joker often finds that others welcome a more genuine and true friendship.

The Caretaker/Gossiper

It would seem strange to classify these two masks together, but both are really of the same basis or foundation. The caretaker mask appears on someone who spends the majority of their time looking after others rather than themselves. They show great concern for others while the gossiper will expend a great deal of energy talking about others. They may often focus on solving other peoples' problems rather than their own.

In both cases, the mask wearer focuses on others to avoid any focus on themselves. They do not allow themselves the time to evaluate their own feelings and needs. Their focus on others is based on a need to avoid themselves coupled with a desire to help others. Many caretakers have defined their self esteem through helping others rather than discovering their inherent reality and goodness.

The Listener

The listener is someone who devotes all of his or her time to listening to other people's problems, desires and goals. Unfortunately, although they may have needs and goals of their own, they hide from expressing these by giving all their attention to others. Although they would like to be listened to, they are fearful of exposing their own values and beliefs for fear of ridicule. In doing so, they have lost the ability to express their inner voice.

The Silent/Hiding Mask

By being silent about our own needs and feelings, we can often avoid confrontation with others. The silent or hiding masks are worn by those who experienced rejection and ridicule earlier in life when they expressed their needs and wants to others. They may have been punished for being assertive and therefore have learned to forego communicating their needs due to the fear of being rejected for making demands on others.

Ironically, another way of hiding is to draw attention to one's self as an authority, by coming up with better answers, or by being different. These attitudes or behaviors keep us from being "just one of the gang" and save us from the feelings we might experience if we felt we weren't fitting in.

In each case our mask protects us from rejection, but we do not fully participate with others, nor are we communicative. While longing for closeness, our silence and hiding mask prevents us from developing the intimacy that we desire.

Generalities of Masks

Keep in mind that none of the above descriptions are meant to be judgmental. They are simply the result of habits we may have developed to hide our emotions and provide defense mechanisms to protect ourselves. At one time these mechanisms may have been necessary and appropriate tools for self defense. Unfortunately, these protection mechanisms may no longer be serving us. We may be living under different circumstances, or the threat may no longer be there, yet by habit we continue to use the protection mechanisms. We need to find a way to change our habits and achieve emotional health.

Many of us may wear one or more of the above masks at varying times. There are times when wearing a mask may be appropriate. Sometimes we meet with individuals whom we may not trust and therefore may prefer to keep certain things close to our chest. We may also find that certain areas of work require a friendly smile or demeanor. The key problem for many mask wearers is the inability to remove or lose the mask at times when sharing may be appropriate or when there really is no threat.

For many of us, our mask has become so much part of our

identity that we are unable to choose to remove the mask even when we might want to. Often we may miss opportunities of closeness because we are so accustomed to maintaining the mask. The mask can be helpful but it can work against us if our behavior and fear prevent us from removing it. If the latter is the case, then we need to accept and feel comfortable with our emotions. This is the key to removing the mask.

Dropping our emotional mask allows others to understand and notice our needs. When we show we are sad or hurt, others can respond to help us. If our mask is in place then others will not know that we are hurting and will not be aware that we need reassurance and help.

Habits of Emotional Avoidance

To keep our emotions at bay, there are a number of techniques that we may use to keep the pain away. Unfortunately, these techniques eventually catch up with us and/or block us from experiencing joy in our lives as well. Emotional avoidance methods can be subtle and we may not be consciously aware of our method of avoiding our feelings. Following is a list of some of the techniques used to avoid emotions and the reality of our lives.

Keeping Busy

By taking on extra responsibilities, whether at work, in our families, or as a volunteer, we end up keeping ourselves so busy that we simply do not have time to feel. There is no balance in our life. We end up rushing around and being unable to slow down. Eventually we can burn out and then need to face the emotions we have been avoiding. Escaping from our emotions by keeping busy dampens the pain but does not allow us to heal.

Keeping the Focus on Others

By focusing on other people's problems we distract ourselves from our own problems and avoid them. We may have a sense of value in helping others, but we are unable to take a close look at ourselves. We may become defensive when someone tries to talk to us about our own problems.

Taking Drugs

Drugs (even prescription drugs) are often used to avoid our feelings. Unfortunately, many of us have resorted to medication to resolve our feelings of sadness. To give us a lift some may take hallucinogenic drugs to alter our perception of our reality. We get a false lift - a false sense of joy. What goes up must come down, so we try to get the feeling again, and end up addicted to a drug and with our emotions unresolved. Facing pain can be difficult. Drugs are often used as a way of avoiding pain.

Drinking Alcohol

Alcohol can work as a suppressant. Having even only an occasional drink or two can end up suppressing or numbing our emotions. When we start to feel, we reach for a drink to soothe and numb our pain, but the emotions are never actually resolved, only masked. Often after a few drinks one may think that one has achieved a greater sense of self and feel more centered. This is due to the fact that alcohol affects our judgment and on a very subtle level, we may be letting some defense down. Some of us may have wonderful sharing experiences under the influence, but the sharing ends once we sober up.

Maintaining Denial

The simplest way to avoid feeling is to maintain a wall of denial saying that "I'm not hurting" or "I'm not angry", even though all the evidence points to the fact that we have unresolved emotions. We may even be so good at denial that we actually believe that we are not hurting.

Maintaining Noise

To keep our minds occupied we will often turn on a television or radio just to fill the silence. Even when we are out in nature we may need some stimulus to keep ourselves and our minds away from our emotions. At home we may have the TV or radio on even if we are not watching or even listening. We simply have it on to fill an emptiness. It becomes background noise. Even when we are out in the woods we may miss the beautiful sounds of nature by bringing a portable stereo. It is possible to achieve a sense of peace with nature. The forests are alive with meditative sounds. If we are running from our emotions it is difficult to sit still and enjoy the peace, so we create some artificial noise to fill the peacefulness. When we begin our recovery, we may find that enjoying the sounds of nature will be healing and peaceful.

Smoking

Emotional depression has also been linked to a number of behavior patterns. Tests have shown that anti-depressants have helped smokers quit. Doctors have noted that smokers who can't quit are more likely to be depressed. Some studies have noted that cigarette smoking affects the chemicals in the brain related to depression.

Compulsive Behaviors

A recent treatment program for compulsive shopping was successful when the patients were treated for their depression rather than for their habit. As adults we seem to develop numerous methods for dealing with depression that do not get to the root of the problem. In many cases, if the depression is treated, the compulsive behavior simply disappears.

Self Abuse

In recent years the medical profession has become aware of various methods of self abuse other than drinking and taking drugs. These forms of self abuse include sexual addictions, self cutting and other behaviors such as hair pulling and physically hitting oneself. These behaviors are often used as a distraction from the emotional pain. The physical pain inflicted through these behaviors allows oneself to focus on something other than the emotional pain. Quite often the person is overwhelmed by emotion and uses this type of behavior for expressing emotion. This method is usually rooted in low self esteem and an inability to express emotions in more constructive and appropriate ways.

The Racing Mind and Obsessing

One way of avoiding emotions is to think obsessively about something or someone. Often we may find our mind racing, resulting in insomnia or an inability to focus on the task at hand. A racing mind is a protection device that either we or our subconscious mind evokes to avoid feelings. If someone is thinking all the time, then they will be experiencing themselves only on an intellectual level and will be blocking out the feelings that are the root of the problem. Simply acknowledging this and slowing down the mind to discover the feelings can often resolve this problem.

Computers and the Internet

One of the greatest inventions in the last few years has been the home computer and the Internet. The Internet has become a valuable resource to many people, and I do not want to undermine its value as a communication tool. Unfortunately, many people spend far too great a time focusing on the computer and its software rather than themselves and their relationships. Some may talk excessively about the hardware and software they are running, which is fine if both parties are truly interested in this subject, but many simply use the topic to avoid the discussion of issues, world problems and their own emotions. With the creation of the Internet, may people spend hours on the IRC chat relays, web surfing and news reading. Some people have begun to recognize the IRC and net surfing as another form of addiction. Some people spend hours on their computer, losing sense of cost, time and other responsibilities.

With hobbies or computers, being knowledgeable about a subject is both interesting to others and rewarding as a hobby if one has a sense of balance in one's life. Not having this balance may indicate an obsession or an inability to focus on other areas of one's life.

Comparing Ourselves to Others

As a form of denial, an emotionally hurting person may try to deny their pain by noticing how others are worse off than themselves. They may take note of someone who, in their eyes, has had a worse time. They then remind themselves that things are better for them. This denial technique is a rational way to get themselves to think that the pain is inappropriate. But each of our circumstances are unique in some way. To expect two people to react exactly the same is not reasonable.

Your troubles and your reaction to them belong to you alone and we should not try to compare our troubles to others to try to make us feel better. Sometimes we may feel guilty for feeling pain or hurt, because our problems may seem insignificant to others. We also may not have been given permission, by ourselves or by others, to feel badly. A powerful analogy is that it does not matter how big the pile of manure is because the smaller pile smells just as bad.

Dissociating

One way of avoiding emotions is to simply tune out what is going on around us. In cases of childhood trauma, dissociation is a common occurrence. Dissociation is now being recognized as a symptom of sexual or childhood abuse rather than a pathological state. Although present in psychiatric patients, it can also occur in the general population. By dissociating from oneself, one becomes more of an observer, less present and less connected with oneself, thus avoiding the possibility of emotional pain or discomfort. The individual who is dissociated may be able to function at certain levels in social and work situations, but may be somewhat disconnected emotionally from day to day living.

Things That Hurt - Our Emotional History

Losses and Gains

Living and dealing with loss is a fact of life. Each of us is born and it is inevitable that we will die. In between our birth and death, we will make friends and lose friends, we will set goals and we may achieve them. Other times we may fail. We will be involved in relationships and we will lose relationships, making way for new ones. We will have sickness and we will have health. We will have financially good times and difficult times as well. In *The Road Less Traveled*, Scott Peck suggests that it is important to accept that life is difficult. Losses are as much a part of life as are gains, however it is usually easier for most of us to deal with the gains.

Gains in themselves can result from losses. Alexander Graham Bell said that "For every door that closes behind us, another door opens." Bell went on to say that often too much time is spent focusing on the closed door, and not enough time on the open one. This is true, however some of us never acknowledge the door that closed behind us as we began a new career, started a new relationship or moved to another city, creating an ungrieved loss.

In *How to Survive the Loss of a Loved One*, authors Colgrove, Bloomfield and McWilliams describe various types of losses. There are inevitable losses (situations in which death or separation is imminent), temporary losses (absences from work, a lover going away for a period of time, a child going away to camp) and some not so obvious losses. There can also be losses related to missed opportunities and mini-losses that may accumulate during a day. Missed telephone calls, a missed connection or not hearing about something we want to attend until it is too late are examples of missed opportunities and mini-losses.

At some time or another we may have experienced multiple losses. When this occurs it is as though the stress of the events is not added, but multiplied. We may require the use of avoidance techniques until we are ready and capable of dealing with the event or events. A number of smaller or seemingly insignificant losses can bring about a depression, especially if they occur around the same time. Even a series of bad luck can bring about a depression or sense of loss. Whatever the loss, we need to allow ourselves to feel the loss and go through the natural process of grieving and healing.

Quite often a loss may not become apparent until later in life. Realizing that we may have been deprived of a happy childhood can be considered a non-obvious loss. There is often no external event that triggers the loss, but an internal realization about the nature of our upbringing. This type of loss is just as real as other types of losses and needs to be felt, expressed and grieved.

Any change in our lifestyle can bring about a sense of loss even if the change ends up being for the better in the long run. Graduating, moving, changes in relationships, a different job are all stressful. Again, the important principle we need to follow to keep ourselves emotionally healthy is to express the emotions that we develop regarding these events.

One of the most difficult and stressful losses to endure occurs when we are placed in a state of limbo. Is the relationship going to end? Am I going to lose my job? Is my health OK? Continually wondering about these and other questions can be more stressful than the event itself. Often when and if the event occurs, a sense of relief is felt because the feeling of not knowing is finally removed. Once the state of limbo ends you can then begin the process of healing and moving on.

In addition to feelings of physical and emotional pain, some of the symptoms of loss are:

anger	anxiety
helplessness	emptiness
lack of concentration	mood swings
despair	changes in energy
loneliness	reduced ambition
proneness to error	guilt
sleep disturbances	changes in sexual drive

The key thing to remember is that all or any of these symptoms are normal for anyone who has experienced a loss. Too often, these feelings are fought rather than expressed and experienced. If you have not had an obvious loss, yet you relate to a number of the above reactions, you might wish to examine your past for a not-so-obvious loss or a series of such losses. Some of the non-obvious losses can be a loss of an ideal or goal, achieving success, moving or similar changes. Learning new things about oneself can also be construed as a loss, especially when it involves a loss of innocence.

Keep in mind that our losses are personal and how we feel may be different than how others may feel. In providing support to the bereaved, counselors are often advised to refrain from saying "I know how you feel". The grieving person has no words to express the rainbow of feelings and thought, that are occurring. It is not possible to match their feelings with our own.

Furthermore, it is important not to compare our losses to those of others. Often people will try to comfort us by saying that someone else may have had troubles that seem worse than ours. I remember being told that at least I had not lost my parents in childhood. This certainly did not help in my grief. In making such statements, others diminish our losses and in doing so, seemingly invalidate the feelings we are having.

Often, too, we may do the comparing of our concerns to those of others in order to deny our own feelings and how we have individually responded to or felt about a particular set of events.

In all losses it is important to feel the loss, to admit that we have lost something and to allow the natural healing process to take place. Often our bodies have begun the healing process without our knowing it. Often we try to block this healing process because we do not understand it or because we do not understand the process of letting go. Colgrove, Bloomfield and McWilliams state that to feel pain after a loss is "normal, natural, proof that you are alive, and a sign that you are able to respond to life's experiences" and "to see pain not as hurting, but healing."

Day to Day Events

Day to day living is not without its minor inconveniences and troubles. A bad day occurs when we have a number of small mishaps. A missed connection or telephone call, poor timing, being splashed by a passing car, or even a minor dent in the car all add up to emotional stress in our lives.

Daily life can be full of annoyances, and we need some outlet to release the emotional tension and stress created by these incidents. If we do not find these outlets for ourselves we end up building a backlog of emotion that adds to our stress level. Eventually we may find that, similar to the phrase "the straw that broke the camel's back", at some point a seemingly insignificant event triggers a flow of emotion. Unfortunately this can be a rather unhealthy method of stress release because we do not have the ability to deal with each issue as it arises. We reduce the level of stress sufficiently to be able to cope but we do not resolve the underlying issues.

Day to day stresses can be viewed as mini-losses that individually might not even be noticed or remembered a few days later, but the stress of the events takes its toll on our emotional health. After a build up of mini-losses we may find ourselves crying unexpectedly or bursting in anger when we can "no longer take it". We may appear somewhat irrational in our behavior because another person viewing our reaction to an event does not know about the little events that have added up to create our discharge. If we maintain healthy emotional habits we will find ways in which we can reduce our emotional tension before we reach our breaking point.

Living, Loving and Learning

Living and sharing with others can bring great joy to our lives, but in doing so we open ourselves to the risk of losing someone for whom we care. With the divorce rate often hovering at the 50 percent level, there are great number of people who have lost their ideal of having a marriage that will last forever. There are many people who are angry and hurt about many things that may have gone wrong in a marriage or relationship. If these life challenges are not resolved, they will be carried into the next relationship or marriage, bringing a greater sensitivity to other issues.

We may often be hurt by people who behave in ways that hurt us. We may be hurt by family members or friends. Some people may do things intentionally, while others may simply be doing things not because they are mean people, but because they do not know better. Others may not have the skills to communicate without attacking. Often someone's behaviors or actions may not coincide with our goals, leaving us frustrated and hurt.

All of us go through breakups and letdowns. We have our successes but we have our failures as well. All of these events that occur in our lives result in emotions being generated that we need to express and resolve. If we resolve the issues then we end up living, loving and forgiving, which brings about learning.

Crimes Against the Heart and Soul

In our own emotional development there are many factors that either facilitate emotional expression or encourage us to avoid it. The causes of our own emotional abandonment are numerous. Some of us were never taught to value our emotions. We may have had poor emotional role models and may have never been taught how to effectively communicate our feelings. In some families, emotional expression may be de-valued and ridiculed, or we may even have been shamed for having emotions. In some cases we may have been hurt so deeply by the actions of others that we choose to avoid our emotions as a way of coping with our pain. Often we may refrain from expressing ourselves when there is a lack of trust or fear that we will be ridiculed. These are crimes of the soul.

In all of the above cases, the shaming of our emotional side is an injury to our soul or heart. These injuries can run deep into our consciousness and affect our emotional state and comfort in expressing ourselves until we re-evaluate the issue. Although we may not be able to recall a specific incident or trauma, an environment of constant shame, scolding or subtle put downs can lead to a demoralized spirit that will likely result in unresolved emotional trauma. This trauma will come to the forefront when later we discover that our treatment was unhealthy, unfair and undeserving, or possibly when we become involved in a relationship.

Another type of emotional abuse or scarring occurs when another person criticizes a child when the child is creatively expressing themselves. Children will freely express themselves through inquiring, wondering and will also artistically express themselves through dancing, singing or playfulness. Often children are robbed of their freedom to express themselves when they are shamed or ridiculed for their spontaneity. Excessive controlling of the child will lead to loss of connection with the creative aspect of themselves.

Actions that ridicule or shame our creative center or that shut down a child's expression of self is a crime against the soul and creativity of the child. The child is taught to suppress the expression of creativity - one of the greatest sources of human joy and expression. Fortunately though, the adult can still find within themselves his or her creative center, and learn to be comfortable in letting his or her creative aspects and talents shine again. Through emotional release and resolution, the person can reconnect and rejuvenate his or her creative personality.

Shame and Guilt

Being given or taking on inappropriate responsibility is another crime of the soul. Children inappropriately are given and accept responsibility for what has happened to them. Many adult children of alcoholics learn through their 12 step programs that they were not responsible for the treatment they received as children. Without any other models, many of these children assumed that their environment and the treatment they were receiving were normal.

Realizing the falseness of the image of their family, and the fact that their environment was not normal, leads the adult child to try to reconcile their past. This usually involves revisiting the past and resolving the fear and pain associated with their upbringing, and then allowing themselves to develop healthier patterns of behavior in their current and future relationships.

Abuse and Trauma

In terms of mental health, there is a strong link between some mental health disorders and childhood trauma. Many victims of trauma suffer from Borderline Personality Disorder, which is characterized by a pervasive pattern of instability of self-image, interpersonal relationships and mood, beginning in early childhood and present in a variety of contexts. Also included in the list of symptoms are a recurrent feeling of emptiness and boredom, as well as self-mutilating behavior.

Pierre Janet suggested as early as 1889 that emotionally intense events are made traumatic when the integration of the experience is interfered with. Janet believed that these intense emotions cause a dissociation of memories from consciousness and result in the memories being stored as anxieties, panic, nightmares, and flashbacks. Janet observed that his patients had difficulty learning from their experience and seemed to focus a great deal of energy on keeping their emotions under control.

In *Therapy for Adults Molested as Children, Beyond Survival*, author J. Briere writes "The diagnosis of Borderline Personality Disorder is a more recent phenomenon." It has been suggested that the label of borderline personality disorder is most commonly placed on patients who exhibit the symptoms of severe post-sexual abuse trauma.

In a paper entitled *Childhood Trauma in Borderline Personality Disorder*, authors Herman, Perry and van der Kolk state that "the role of childhood trauma, including parental abuse, in the development of this disorder has received less systematic attention". In three small studies, the data suggested that in borderline patients, a history of childhood abuse may be common.

In other studies of borderline patients, up to 75 percent of the patients had experienced incest. In another study of psychiatric patients, it was found that eight of 12 patients diagnosed as borderline had a history of childhood abuse (Herman). A study by Brier found that 12 of 14 patients had experienced abuse before the age of 16.

Authors Herman, Perry and van der Kolk state that "The great majority of subjects with definite borderline personality disorder gave histories of major childhood trauma; 71 percent had been sexually abused, and 62 percent had witnessed domestic violence." According to the study, borderline patients had suffered from abuse more often than others and also reported more types of trauma. These abuses and trauma often began in early childhood and were repetitive, resulting in high trauma scores.

In the cases of children who have been abused emotionally or psychologically, or who have witnessed abuse, there is likely to be a greater degree of mental health issues than those who have not. It is interesting to note that repeated abuse results in a higher total trauma score than for those with singular abusive experiences. This seems to validate the idea that prolonged emotional abuse can be equally damaging as other childhood traumas. It is this emotional abuse that may leave us numb and unable to express our emotions later as adults. The combined effect of numerous incidents of emotional abuse may lead to similar symptoms of repressed emotions, numbness and the irrational thinking that comes with unresolved issues and loss of our inherent nature.

Often it is not until later in life that we may realize the impact of our upbringing or realize that our family situation may have been abusive. Often, as children, we come to accept our environment simply because we know of no other standard of behavior. We do not know that in other families, parents are supportive and nurturing. As children we may understand that we are in pain, but do not have the words or understanding to deal with the emotional injury until we become adults. The fact that our needs as children were rarely met may bring about emotional pain and habitual patterns in our adult life. Through emotional and healing work we can free ourselves of these patterns and resolve the pain that has lingered below the surface of consciousness for so long.

In life it is not pain that causes insanity, but the lies we tell ourselves about the pain. These lies are often sometimes the only way we know of coping through the pain. Fortunately, we are able to heal by beginning to tell ourselves the truth about our pain, accepting it and letting go of it.

Recognizing Abuse

In *Toxic Parents*, Dr. Susan Forward writes about the various types of abuse that occur in families. Due to the lack of a standard to compare our own family life, we may not realize until later in life that our family upbringing or a relationship was not normal and that it was, in fact, abusive. Inadequate parents, controllers, hinderers, alcoholics, verbal abusers, physical abusers, and sexual abusers all perpetrate a crime on an innocent victim who often feels shame, blame and low self-esteem.

Following are the characteristics of abusive types that we may encounter. Keep in mind that many of these characteristics can be applied to spouses, employers, friends, and other members of the community as well.

The Inadequate: Inadequate parents are those who are so focused on their own world that they can pay little attention to their children. The parents are often overly sensitive and cannot deal with any criticism. These parents often make excuses for themselves and hide their problems with statements such as "we're doing the best we can". Inadequate parents often lack listening skills and have not experienced their own emotional development.

Controllers: Controllers often experience a fear of letting go. They often believe that their children were created to serve them and that they own their children as possessions. The children are not allowed to develop their own set of standards or values and have difficulty exercising decision-making skills due to guilt and manipulation by the parents.

Addicts and Alcoholics: Alcoholics and addicts often make promises that are not kept. Denial of problems, mood swings, inconsistency, and blaming are all characteristics of an alcoholic home. Keep in mind that the drinking is only one of many symptoms of an alcoholic. Many parents could be considered to be dry alcoholics, who have given up the drink but do not have the skills to nurture and assist in problem solving. Since addictions tend to follow family patterns, children of alcoholics tend to develop certain characteristics often referred to as para-alcoholism as a result of their conditions of upbringing.

The Verbal Abusers: Verbally abusive parents often try to motivate children with disrespectful comments. They can be verbally direct, or their comments may be subtly abusive. Abusive statements may be in the form of comparisons to others or subtle put downs of choices of clothing, friends or interests. The parents exhibit a great degree of insensitivity and rob the children of autonomy and self-confidence. Challenging the parent often leads to denial and attempts by the parent to make the child feel guilty.

The Hinderers: The hinderer is someone who says or does things that hinder our development and maturity process. Hinderers do not provide us with the guidance we require to develop our sense of worth and autonomy. They also go further by saying things that erode our confidence and trust in our decision-making abilities. Hinderers instill self doubt and discourage the development of our interests and thus our opportunities to socialize.

The Physical Abusers: Physical abusers are those who use physical force to control or harm their children. The parent may often apologize for the strike, placing the child in an awkward and difficult situation of being expected to love and forgive an abuser. Physical abuse may also occur as threats, in which a domineering parent may behave in a manner that threatens the safety of the child. Physical abusers often have not learned the skills necessary to cope with their anger. Although they may express remorse, they do not have the skills to control their actions in times of anger.

The Sexual Abusers: Sexual abuse has always been more prevalent than society would care to admit. Freud was astounded by the number of clients who described sexual abuse. Sexual abuse is not limited to unwanted touching or intercourse. Sexual abuse involves power and a lack of respect for a child's innocence. Abuse can be in the form of inappropriate comments, exposure or teasing. Abused children often experience a myriad of problems later in life that they may not attribute to the earlier abuse.

Other types of abuse include verbal abuse disguised as jokes; withholding approval or attention to gain power; being put down for having a different point of view; discounting your achievements or feelings; accusing and blaming; and denial of the fact that their actions hurt you.

Often an abuser will use various blocking techniques to avoid accountability for their actions. Examples of blocking are statements such as "it was only meant in fun", "I was only joking", or "you're too sensitive". These are statements that deny that abuse is occurring and puts the onus on the victim to change. Emotional wounding occurs when we are shamed, ridiculed, lack nurturance, or are humiliated.

The Impact of Trauma

Psychologists are now learning about the impact a traumatic event can have on the lives of people who experience them. Either as a victim of a crime or as a witness to a crime, people can be profoundly affected by an event that may only last a few seconds. A robbery, injustice or even an accident can leave us feeling shaken and upset. Often such events will trigger a re-evaluation of ourselves. Recently a friend of mine was present when a bank was robbed. Although not physically harmed, she was quite shaken and almost in a state of shock.

Victims of robberies feel violated and often experience periods of fear and insomnia afterwards. Often, victims of sexual assault and rape will experience a complete change in their emotional chemistry. Victims often feel anger and resentment and experience a myriad of behavioral issues as a result of a trauma. A sense of violation and loss of security and safety may permeate their daily lives.

In a Letter to the Editor of the Ottawa Citizen, Erica Saunders describes the pain and emotional trauma experienced as a victim of an attempted rape:

> "I am a survivor of a violent rape attempt. I am usually a sweet, caring, sensitive person. These days I am totally the opposite. I am like a wild wounded animal. If there is a way to destroy a woman in fifteen minutes this is it. First you have to deal with policemen, then doctors, then yourself. In two weeks I lost 15 pounds. I still have problems with food. He touched me; I feel dirty; I take four to five showers a day. It was an unprovoked attack... I was robbed of my rights, left to deal with a rainbow of unwanted feelings."

Obviously, such traumas involve much more pain than the physical trauma. The emotional trauma can last for months and even years. Both psychiatrists and psychologists now understand the impact that rape or childhood sexual abuse has on adult lives. These victims may experience difficulty in relationships and in situations requiring trust, long after the event has occurred.

Traumatic Events and Delayed Reaction

In some cases the effects of the event may not be felt for months or years. This delayed reaction is actually quite common. In a book about Post Traumatic Stress Disorder (PTSD) called *Aftershock*, Andrew E. Slaby tells us that "Many of us have had aftershock experiences, going through the first stages of a crisis numb and in shock, only to wake up one morning a few days, weeks or even months later in tears, the full impact of what happened finally hitting home".

In many cases, a period of change, emotional pain, or loss can leave us with the same conditions and symptoms of PTSD. In cases of PTSD, the cause of the symptoms is the inability to process what has happened to us. As with any emotional trauma, we need to cognitively and emotionally process the event. In PTSD, failure to process the event results in the event being frozen in time, with a need to repeat our story. Often similar situations and events will trigger a heightened sense of emotion and fear, often referred to as re-stimulation. More often than not, at this time in the process, the telling of the story does not relieve the symptoms but heightens the intense feelings and behaviors

According to the *Diagnostic and Statistical Manual of Mental Disorders* (DSM-IV) which is a psychiatrist's diagnostic tool, PTSD symptoms involve: efforts to avoid thoughts or feelings associated with the trauma; efforts to avoid activities or situations that arouse recollections of the trauma; inability to recall an important aspect of the trauma (psychogenic amnesia); marked diminished interest in significant activities; feeling of detachment or estrangement from others; restricted range of affect (unable to have feelings); sense of foreshortened future (i.e. does not expect to have a career, marriage, or children, or a long life).

PTSD may also involve difficulty falling or staying asleep; irritability or outbursts of anger; difficulty concentrating; hyper-vigilance; exaggerated startle response; physiologic reactivity upon exposure to events that symbolize or resemble an aspect of the traumatic event. With PTSD, some people may find themselves over responding to a sound, sight or smell that reminds them, even if only very subtly, of the event. Due to the heightened emotional sensitivity and anxiety, some turn to substance abuse or other forms of emotional denial. This is also true for many children who experience a troublesome or traumatic childhood.

Although the definition of PTSD was developed as a result of the problems of Vietnam war veterans, its implication is much wider. The former definition of trauma for PTSD is "an event that is outside the range of usual human experience and that would be markedly distressing to almost anyone, e.g. serious threat to one's life or physical integrity; serious threat or harm to one's children, spouse or other close relatives and friends; or seeing another person who has recently been, or is being, seriously injured or killed as the result of an accident or physical violence."

If we examine this definition we find that if a person experiences a number of stressful events at once, this could be considered outside of the range of usual human experience. This would be markedly distressing to almost anyone. It is quite likely that a period of intense stress could bring about PTSD symptoms. The newer DSM criteria for PTSD has been changed. The definition of trauma is an event that was directly experienced, witnessed or learned about that threatened the victim's life or physical integrity. In addition, the requirement of being outside the range of human experience has been removed, as it was too restrictive. Also, a new category called acute stress disorder has been added, recognizing the fact that many people are adversely affected by overwhelmingly stressful events.

Studies have shown that 60 percent of persons with symptoms of mental disorder had suffered some sort of trauma two weeks before any illness appeared. In the months following a traumatic event, the risk of suicide is six times greater and the risk of depression is twice as great as prior to the event. Furthermore, PTSD has mostly been related to adults, but the symptoms of PTSD are often present in adults who experience abuse earlier in life. Children are considered to be very susceptible to PTSD since they have not yet developed the ability to express themselves in words, yet have developed the ability to remember feelings and sounds. Often the trauma will be stored as memory with no words to describe the trauma.

Since children do not have the understanding and rational capabilities to deal with events, the way they develop explanations of events is very different from adults. If they are harmed, they will not likely have the words and understanding to articulate the hurt. Since psychogenic amnesia is one of the symptoms of PTSD, it is likely that children will bury away the memories until they are ready to understand and deal with them.

In addition, while children can be extremely perceptive, their ability to attribute events to their understanding of the world may be undeveloped and based on fantasy. To an adult, divorce or separation may seem an acceptable resolution to a problem. To a young child this may be seen as an extremely threatening and frightening event that shatters their sense of security and safety.

As adults we often experience events that are outside the scope of our ability to deal with at the time. While PTSD was originally used to describe the symptoms of Vietnam veterans, it has implications for those of us who grew up in what seemed like a war zone. Although we may not be classified as having PTSD according to the DSM-III or DSM-IV, we may be exhibiting all or some of the symptoms due to the troubles we have experienced.

I believe that the determination of PTSD should not be a yes or no answer, but measured on a continuum or scale based on the individual's rating of the event and the subsequent impact of the event on the person's life.

In the year after graduating from University I experienced a substantial number of health problems, change and losses. Although I was not a veteran from military service, I certainly felt that I was a veteran of my own personal war to survive those times. Those events were outside the scope of what one person might be expected to endure. Given that some people are stronger than others and therefore seem to struggle through a greater load, the definition of PTSD should be varied according to the individual's ability.

These events led to a process of redefinition of myself. Four years later, I found I had not dealt with the events, was emotionally numb and experiencing a number of problems. Revisiting the events, expressing the emotion and completing the processing of these and other events restored a sense of sanity and ability to relate with myself and others. I now consider these events to be part of my personal history, rather than unresolved issues that generate pain and emotional discomfort.

To resolve symptoms of PTSD, one needs to re-visit the trauma and process the experience and feelings in safety. As with any emotional trauma it is helpful to find suitable professional help and assistance through friends and support groups.

Mark Linden O'Meara

Emotions and Memory

A Forgotten Past

Memory and Pride were fighting.
Memory said, "It was like that,"
and Pride said "It couldn't have been"
And Memory gave in...
> \- Nietzsche

This statement by Nietzsche reflects the tug-of-war that our consciousness can play with regard to the recall of traumatic or distressing events or times in our lives. I find Neitzsche's words also provide insight into the denial of those who are accused of abusing or of those who were present during situations in which unpleasantness occurred. With these people, it is pride that keeps them from admitting the true nature of their own experience. It is difficult for them to admit that things were a certain way.

For the survivor of abuse, amnesia often occurs. In my own case, I had forgotten numerous aspects of my own childhood. My own repression of painful memories was due to the simple logic of "out of sight, out of mind, out of memory, no more pain." But had I really forgotten, or simply repressed them? There is a distinction between the two. Due to the emotionally painful nature of the events, I was unable to bring those events and the associated affect into my present existence for to do so would have taxed my coping resources beyond my capabilities. In order to protect myself, my mind kept them in my subconscious. The price of doing so was a heightened state of anxiety and emotional numbness.

Voluntary attempts at recalling my childhood did not bring about any memories. It was the development of appropriate support and community, and the acceptance of my emotions in a safe place, that eventually brought about the recall of my memory. This recall occurred little by little, like flashbulb experiences, one at a time. As this occurred, my self understanding grew accordingly.

I have learned that my experience is not unique. Many adult children report that once they start on their path of emotional recovery, they begin to remember events they had previously seemingly forgotten. In my own experience of recovery I have met numerous people who have retrieved memories that were put away long ago.

It is also possible to forget the nuances of a situation as well. We may forget severely traumatizing events, however, we may also repress memories of how things were in a household or relationship. The tone of the environment may be repressed to avoid dealing with our emotional state at the time. For a long time I had forgotten how depressed my mother was when I was a teenager. Both my parents refused to admit they had problems. I had forgotten how my teenage environment had been contaminated with my parents' depression, helplessness, inability to cope, and a sense of extreme emotional sensitivity.

In Freud's earlier days as a psychotherapist, he developed the theory that conflict was the key to repression. The conflict may arise when the view one holds of oneself is different or incongruent with the truth of an event. Other conflicts, such as how one views a parent versus how one "should" view a parent, can result in memory conflict as the child or adult is torn between the two images. A person with a tyrannical parent may feel fear and anger towards the parent. This would conflict with the injunction that one should love their parents.

Prior to the work of Freud, two well know philosophers, Arthur Schopenhauer and Johann Herbart, wrote about our unwillingness to discuss or face unpleasant circumstances that harm our current interests and views of ourselves. Freud and Dr. Josef Breuer concluded that some people actively attempt to push memories that have deep emotional meaning and impact below the surface of their consciousness as a method of avoidance and sometimes of survival. Freud believed that repressed memories affected our behavior and emotions and in the end produced disorders.

Recent studies have indicated that we may possess two memory systems - one explicit and one implicit. Explicit memory deals with conceptual, factual and verbal information as well as conscious and reflective awareness. The implicit memory deals with conditioned emotional response, skills and habits, sensormotor skills, and unconscious and non-reflective awareness. Under stress, the explicit system is impeded while the implicit system becomes more robust.

At the present time, we do not fully understand the role that emotions play in memory nor vice versa, although progress is being made in this area. There are some theories that suggest that memory may in fact be emotion. In 1995, Wendy E. Hovdestad and Connie M. Kristiansen of Carleton University studied over 200 female survivors of child sexual abuse. The study focused on the experiences, memory and recovery process. The findings of the study were consistent with other studies in that approximately half of survivors report some memory loss or disruption. Other studies have put this number between 59 and 64 percent. In this study, of the 51 women who reported recovered memories, over 62 percent reported that their memory returned during therapy.

The Carleton University study questioned the participants on which of 12 events had triggered the return of their memories. The study reported the following as the most prevalent triggers:

Before having any therapy:

An event similar to the original trauma	31.3%
Beginning an important relationship	30.1%
Watching a film or reading about sexual abuse	20.7%
Parenting	20.5%
A creative process	15.7%

While participants were in therapy:

A support group	47.6%
A creative process	41.7%
Watching/reading about abuse	36.6%
Beginning an important relationship	27.7%
An event similar to the trauma	22.9%
Stopping alcohol or drugs	15.9%
Ending a significant relationship	13.4%

In *Mind Meets Body: On the Nature of Recovered Memories of Trauma*, authors Hovdestad and Kristiansen write about compelling evidence that memory is multimodal. They state that we possess memory systems, one of which we are aware, the other operating without our awareness. Hovdestad and Kristiansen write that "Trauma causes alterations in the production and release of stress-responsive neurochemicals such as norepinephrine and the endogenous opiods, and extreme levels of these neurochemicals disrupt everyday explicit information processing. The implicit processing system, however, continues to function in the face of trauma."

Recent studies of amnesia and trauma victims have indicated that the emotional valence of an experience affects recall accuracy. Recurrent observations of traumatic memories indicate that these memories are stored differently than declarative memory, perhaps due to the extreme emotional arousal. In a study by Briere and Elliot, significant degrees of traumatic amnesia were reported for virtually all forms of trauma. Numerous studies have also shown that the age at which the abuse occurs as well as the frequency of the abuse are related to the occurrence of traumatic amnesia. Traumatic amnesia will more likely occur if the trauma took place at a younger age or if the event was prolonged.

In the concluding paragraphs of *Dissociation and the Fragmentary Nature of Traumatic Memories*, Van der Kolk and Fisler write:

"Recently we collaborated in a neuroimaging symptom provocation study of some of the subjects who were part of the memory study reported here. When these subjects had their flashbacks in the laboratory, there was significantly increased activity in the areas in the right hemisphere that are associated with the processing of emotional experiences, as well as in the right visual association cortex. At the time there was significantly decreased activity in Broca's area, in the left hemisphere. These findings are inline with the results of this study: that traumatic "memories" consist of emotional and sensory states, with little verbal representation. In other work we have hypothesized that, under conditions of extreme stress, the hippocampally based memory categorization system fails, leaving memories to be stored as affective and perceptual states."

A question that faces us when we start to remember incidents from our past is why do we recall some memories but forget others. What are the processes and conditions that cause us to forget or put away memories and what bring them back? In *Unlocking the Secrets of Your Childhood Memories*, authors Dr. Kevin Leman and Randy Carlson suggest that the answer is simply that "People remember only those events from early childhood that are consistent with their present view of themselves and the world around them". The authors call this the law of creative consistency. "Without consistency", they write, " you'd be in deep trouble. It is your God-given ability to keep the present and past in balance so that you don't fall over the edge into frustration, depression or insanity."

Facilitating Memory Recall

In the case of memory recall there are a number of factors that seem to facilitate the remembering of events. The first factor is the creating of a safe or comfortable environment. This may occur simply by beginning to accept the start of a healing process or by joining a support group. Secondly, memory recall usually occurs after the acknowledgment and recall of the emotion. The notion that memory reappearance will precede the emotion appears to be the reverse of what happens. Usually a cue of some sort will trigger the emotion and once the emotional expression is facilitated the memory surfaces and reveals itself.

In *Unchained Memories, True Tales of Traumatic Memories Lost and Found*, author Lenore Terr, M.D. writes that "In order for a repressed memory to return, there usually is a ground -that is a general emotional state and a cue". It is often this cue, that may be only a smell, taste, a simple reminder by way of a similar experience, or any cue from our senses. Terr suggests that vision is one of the strongest cues. Additionally, I believe that a visual cue, as seen through the mind's eye, can also act as a strong stimulus.

The nature of traumatic memories has been controversial as well as difficult to study. The recall of abuse often leads to confronting the abuser or realizing the true nature of individuals who have been close to us. Claims of abuse are often denied, however in some cases, full confessions and apologies have been given by the alleged abusers.

In times of recall, individuals like myself may experience self-doubt about the memories. It is often important to remind oneself that although one may be experiencing self-doubt, one is also experiencing a great deal of affect which likely has a basis in some event. If the emotion is processed, the nature of the event will be revealed to us when we are ready.

In recovering memories it is important to understand and accept the ability of our mind to protect us until we are ready to remember. A flood of memories could be overwhelming. Our mind is truly our ally in times of memory retrieval as I have heard many times from 12-step group members. It seems that the emotion and memory will bubble to the surface as we are ready to face and process these memories. Although the memories and emotion may feel overwhelming, our subconscious mind seems to instinctively know that we have developed sufficient resources and support to work through the trauma.

In one instance of recall my memories were trigger by a bloody nose. While trying to loosen a part underneath my van, my wrench slipped and struck me on the nose. As I crawled out from under the van, I found myself experiencing memories of being punched in the nose by the grade eight class bully, who had at the time cornered me in a backyard and was threatening me. As the memory came back, so too did the feelings of rejection, anger and fear that were going through my mind at the time of the incident. Fortunately, at the time of recall, I knew enough about emotional processing to accept the feelings and release them.

Dealing with painful memories can consume a great deal of energy and personal resources. The key to retrieving these memories is the awareness and acceptance of what we are feeling.

Emotional Processing

Each of us get hurt to varying degrees simply by living our lives. No one is immune to difficulties. How we deal with these emotional challenges greatly affects our future responses to similar events and challenges. I believe, as many others do, that a great deal of mental illness results from the inability to process emotions and the associated events.

Each time we experience an event that triggers an emotion, we have the choice of experiencing and processing the emotion or avoiding it. As we process the emotions, the energy dissipates and the event is converted to knowledge, information and part of our experience of living. If we do not emotionally process events and feelings, then we will become more sensitive to similar events and issues. Unresolved events become triggers. When we encounter a similar experience, the original emotion is triggered.

Recently, a model of emotional behavior was explained to me by a Zen monk. She told me that these ideas have been a fundamental of Zen practice for over 2500 years. The model shows us how our emotions and the way we think build habitual patterns of behavior and self talk that appear in our conscious daily living. The model shows the levels of emotional integration: the event or condition; emotional expression or non-expression; self-talk, frozen needs, beliefs and attitudes; habits, patterns and behaviors; and consciousness.

Events and Conditions

Events and conditions in our daily lives trigger our thoughts and feelings. The triggering event or condition is the first in a series of levels in the model. Day to day events, family conditions, stress, and upsetting events, as well as the positive events will all lead to the next stage of this model sometimes without our own awareness. Even if we do not intellectually acknowledge the event or condition, we notice that an event has occurred because of our emotional reaction. If we are consciously aware of our emotional response then we will more likely express our feelings. We may acknowledge the event on a very subtle level.

Often a reaction to an event or condition may not occur until years after the original event. We may gain the insight that a particular event affected us in ways we did not understand at the time. We may realize that the way we were treated was unfair or perhaps we may develop different standards. When we look back at an event we may feel anger or sadness, even though we may not have felt these emotions at the time of the event. This is quite common as we mature and begin to understand what kind of relationships we want in life, and as we begin to learn more about issues such as dependency, addictions or general dysfunction in relationships and friendships. After reading *Toxic Parents* by Dr. Susan Forward, I realized the nature of my parents' behavior. I then became angry at my parents because of the new understanding I had developed. I had not felt angry at the time that some of these events occurred.

Emotional Reaction

This stage occurs as our body and emotional center react with sadness, joy, anger, or other appropriate responses to an event or condition. In a positive emotional climate we will likely feel free and encouraged to express ourselves. Alternately, in negative emotional climates we may feel it necessary to bottle the expression of emotion. Both emotional expression and avoidance lead to the next stage of our emotional model, but with different consequences.

Denial of the event or condition at this point does not halt the development of emotions, self-talk, attitudes, or behaviors. The event is simply pushed out of our conscious thinking, and results in subtle forms of anxiety, tension, stress, and sensitivity. We end up using energy to keep these thoughts of the event out of our current thinking patterns. This emotional blocking results in an accumulation of emotional "baggage". Later, because we have not dealt with the original issue, we become sensitive to similar events or conditions. These issues become trigger points that cause us to react not only to the current situation, but with the affect, attitudes and fears associated with the original and other similar incidents we have experienced.

In a nurturing environment we will be more likely to express our emotions. We will experience a sense of validation and being listened to. This helps us to develop positive self talk, attitudes and self-esteem. In a non-nurturing environment we may learn to view ourselves, our emotional expression and our behavior as shameful and bad. The Eastern approach to emotional numbness is that an individual is still feeling the emotions at a mind-body level. This blocking of the felt sense requires a substantial amount of energy. It is similar to keeping a car still by pressing on both the gas pedal and the brakes at the same time. The car does not move, but considerable energy is spent creating opposing forces. This energy could certainly be used in more purposeful ways!

Self Talk, Frozen Needs and Attitudes

From our own emotional reactions we move to a more conscious level of self talk, frozen needs and attitudes. Once we begin to process our experience of an event and the emotion associated with it, we then begin to filter the event through our own experiences and beliefs. Through filtering and association we develop ideas and images of ourselves and others that become part of our way of thinking and eventually part of our behavior and attitudes.

Self talk is the little voice inside our head that churns over ideas and thoughts and advises us whether we can accomplish something or whether we should take risks. Our mind's voice is a part of our consciousness. Unfortunately, our ability to effectively reason is often limited by our emotional baggage or by emotional experiences that we have not resolved. Our voice may indicate fear or rejection, a decision to avoid an issue. Often it is a voice that tells us of our own self worth. If we have often been harmed or abused and have not resolved these emotional issues, we will avoid getting close to others.

Often our self talk can be very subtle and we may not be aware of its tone and effect. We may have a subtle feeling or symbol of ourselves that is of low worth, or of someone who does not deserve love. If we have been nurtured or have accepted events in our lives we will experience self talk that celebrates our talents and has a firm belief in our worthiness.

Too often though, we experience events that challenge our self-esteem and sense of security. These human needs are shared by all. They are needs such as food, shelter, companionship, a sense of belonging, and the need to express our caring for others. As humans, it is natural to seek the love and approval of others. If, on a repeated basis, we are denied the love or approval we need then we may develop what is called a frozen need. Frozen needs are unresolved wants or needs that were not met at some time in our lives.

If at a time we were unable to be close to others, then one may develop a strong need for closeness. This becomes a pattern that permeates new and old friendships and usually results in a feeling that nothing is ever enough. This may occur with financial matters as well. If we experienced times of financial hardship, we may try to ensure that we gather as much as possible. The searching that we do in order to fulfill these frozen needs can lead us on a path of feeling somewhat empty at times, even though we may have attained a degree of closeness and financial success. Later on in our lives we often go about trying to fulfill these needs through relationships, addictions or by trying to obtain the validation we did not receive. We may also develop patterns of behavior that shield us from our pain or inadequacies.

Similar to frozen needs are the attitudes we develop as a result of our self-talk and the messages we may hear from others. Although we may be able to state some of our attitudes verbally, many of our attitudes are a felt sense that we may not be able to put into words. As described in numerous texts on learning, attitudes each have a cognitive, affective and behavioral aspect. The cognitive aspect of an attitude often deals with consistency. We get what we expect and in some ways we expect what we get. The affective aspect refers to feelings associated with the attitude. Events that trigger feelings will lead to attitudes associated with those feelings. Simply working on our behavior or thoughts is not sufficient in effecting attitude change. It is necessary to examine and resolve our feelings regarding the attitude as well.

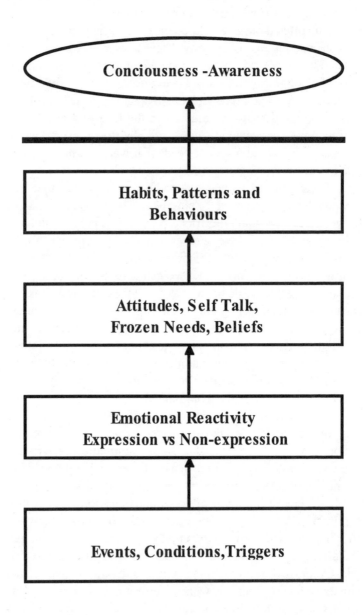

I've heard many people say "I know I'm a nice person, but I just don't feel it."

Habits, Patterns and Behaviors

Our behaviors are often based on expectations, attitudes and our previous responses in similar situations. Often we are unaware of our frozen needs and attitudes and therefore are not in control of our behavior. The development of awareness of our own attitudes, frozen needs and the emotions inherent in them is a major step in our healing process. What are our behavioral responses to the events and conditions we encounter in daily challenges? Are we open to constructive criticism? Are we afraid of expressing our anger? Can we express our love? Do we run from pain and attempt to seek solace in drugs, alcohol or other masking behaviors? Do we recognize that if we work through our pain that it will pass?

Clearly our beliefs about our ability to cope with pain will impact our response. If we are secure in our self worth and abilities, we are more likely to feel comfortable in expressing love and accepting criticism. If we are less secure, we are likely to be defensive and less open. As we have understood with frozen needs, our behavior will often be a reflection of our emotional state and learned behaviors. We may constantly seek to fulfill a particular need or we may choose relationships that seem to fulfill a need. Our habits and patterns of behavior are, more often than not, a manifestation of our unresolved emotions and attitudes. In many cases, unresolved issues will lead to addictions, compulsive behavior, anxieties, and running from closeness. We may be triggered and react strongly when encountering familiar issues. We may do things to cover up or rationalize our reaction, leading to further anxiety. In every irrational action there is usually one thread of rationality for the behavior.

These unprocessed experiences will help shape our behavior and actions. Furthermore, each incident, if not dealt with emotionally, will result in a loss of connection with our emotional self, increasing our capacity for irrational thinking and reactive behavior. Fortunately, if we begin to examine our emotional issues and start to work on them, it is possible to reconnect with our sense of rationality. The emotional energies that surround the self can be expressed and resolved, thus freeing ourselves to be more creative, clear and aware. One by one, the strands of emotion that cover the self will be peeled away and will no longer be troublesome to us. They will simply become part of our experience and understanding.

I recently spoke with a man at a library while doing some readings on residential school syndrome. As we talked, tears welled up in his eyes as he told me some of the things that he went through during his years as a child and teenager at a residential school. Only now was he beginning to understand the impact of the abuse he had experienced. He spoke of two failed marriages, low self esteem and alcohol problems. Clearly he did not blame the abusers for the failed marriages, but he now had an understanding of the effect of the abuse on his self-esteem and emotional state, which resulted in behaviors that harmed his marriages. Since he had uncovered the underlying issue, he could now begin his healing process. He now had new options, choices and the possibility of doing things differently.

Understanding and acknowledging the impact of an event is a major step in the healing process. It can also be an act of self-acceptance and self-love to forgive oneself for a lower than desired performance in areas of one's life. I have always felt ashamed of my poor academic performance in my last year of high school. I recognize now that I was grieving the loss of a classmate who died when he was hit by a car. I had not previously recognized the depth of the issues I was dealing with at the time and the impact it had on my performance.

In the introduction of this book, you may recall how I described myself prior to my healing work. I kept myself extremely busy, took on many projects and kept myself at a considerable distance from others. I could not slow down, nor could I let people assist me at times when I needed help. I was very independent, and unable to let other people know my true self. I believe that many of these issues were the result of not having processed the natural emotions that had occurred due to the losses I had experienced and the beliefs I developed about myself in the course of my upbringing. As I began to challenge these beliefs and to express and resolve the affect, my self talk improved and I gradually learned new behaviors as a renewed sense of creativity and rationality appeared.

Triggers

Most textbooks on learning describe the effects of stimulus and response. The same theories apply to our emotions as well. The theories of learning state that when two ideas are experienced together, the later presentation of one would trigger the recall of the other. Therefore if, in our own experience, a situation results in a certain response, similar situations will trigger similar responses.

I recently became aware of one of my own triggers and have begun to replace my previous behaviors with a more effective and rewarding pattern. In my family it took a great deal of courage to ask for the most basic things. Since the reaction of my mother would be inconsistent, approaching her usually resulted in a feeling of apprehension and fear. As learning theory would predict, I developed a fear of approaching people or bringing up my own needs.

Another phenomenon of conditioning is the concept of extinction. Extinction refers to an unlearning and progressive weakening of the response. Contrary to the belief that we must work hard at changing one's behavior, extinction can occur rapidly when the unconditioned stimulus is removed and replaced with another. If the stimulus is repeated without the original response, the conditioned association undergoes a weakening. If a new behavior replaces the old one or we do not respond in the same manner, we will experience a change in our behavior or paired emotion.

Since my father was an authoritarian, and somewhat dictatorial, I learned to fear authority figures. I developed awareness of my conditioned response, and recognized that other authority figures could be nurturing and act as mentors. When I encountered an authority figure, I would intercept my thoughts and intervene with a positive and re-affirming statement regarding authority figures. This lead to a reduction in my fear of authority figures and helped me let others begin to nurture me.

Just as conditioned responses trigger our feelings, so do our unresolved emotions. Similar situations will remind us of the paired feelings of the situation. Although we can work on changing our thoughts to avoid certain feelings, it is necessary to resolve the energy associated with the emotions so that the issue is resolved at a deeper level. Otherwise we will constantly have to challenge our thoughts and responses.

Developing Emotional Awareness

The Process of Releasing

Releasing our unresolved emotions involves passing through a number of stages in order to completely release the emotional energy that has been trapped inside us. Furthermore, these stages may be repeated a number of times in the process of freeing our emotions and healing. Often we may not be aware of what originally triggered the emotion. What we may only know is that we are hurting for some unknown reason. We need to move through these moods and feelings and simply allow them to surface and be felt.

The process of healing is also a repetitive process. It involves becoming aware of certain feelings and releasing them, then becoming aware of other feelings and releasing them as well, and so on until we become emotionally clear. This process can take some time, but if we are committed to our emotional health and put some effort into changing our ways to achieve a release we can begin to realize the benefits relatively quickly.

The release process is also a repetitive one. We get in touch with our unresolved emotions one layer at a time. When we achieve release, we essentially peel away a layer of the unresolved emotions. We can then move on to the next layer of emotion and become aware of it when we are ready.

First Awareness

When we are ready, our minds will allow us to gradually begin feeling the emotions that we have been suppressing. Our mind is our own powerful ally and it will protect us from emotions that we are not yet ready to face. Sometimes we need to learn a few lessons, build sufficient strength or gain certain skills before we are ready to deal with our issues. Our subconscious mind is smart enough to know when we are ready and when we are not.

When ready, we will likely begin to experience brief or fleeting moments of sadness, anger or fear. This is likely a signal to us that we are ready to start to feel again and that there is some unresolved emotion to deal with. As quickly as the emotion surfaces in the early stages of release, it may just as quickly disappear. Our mind at this time is probably telling us that there is something to be worked on. The first feelings may come to us like a wave, then disappear.

A reasonable reaction might be to try to hide or to run from these feelings. If we can understand that getting in touch with these feelings and releasing them will bring us greater benefits in the long run, then we will not fall into our old habits of hiding from them. The emotions we touch on may seem intense and frightening to us. We may want to focus on the fact that it must take a tremendous amount of energy to keep these emotions below the conscious level. Think of all the energy that is being used to hold these feelings in place and how that energy could be put to better use!

At this time it is important that we do not dismiss or reject our feelings. It is important that we validate our feelings and take ownership of them. We must remind ourselves that, given our situation and events which occurred in our lives and how we dealt with them, our feelings are reasonable and appropriate.

First awareness of emotions may involve a state of confusion. As we become aware of emotions we may feel as though we are receiving a number of jumbled signals. Slowly we will begin to understand those signals and identify what emotions they are and learn to articulate what we are feeling.

It is important to note that there is a significant difference between logical understanding of an event and experiential understanding. In other words, there is a great difference between talking about our emotions and expressing them. We may logically understand and rationalize events, reactions and other peoples' actions, but to experientially understand means to emotionally accept and let go of the event and feeling so that our inherent nature is no longer affected by the issue. Facing our emotional issues will allow us to integrate events into our lives and bring us closer to others.

In the early stages of awareness we may also begin to remember certain events in our lives that we had long forgotten. These events, like our emotions, may have been kept out of our consciousness due to the painful nature of the events or, as mentioned earlier, the conditions under which the events occurred. It can be quite common to find that memories from our childhood, previously forgotten, can come back with their associated emotions. If we do find ourselves remembering events or incidents, it is because we are ready to deal with these aspects of our lives that we may not have previously dealt with.

Awareness of our emotions can also come to us in our dreams as well as through events in our daily lives. Typically, dreams in which there is water coming up from a sewer, or a river overflowing, indicate that our emotions are a source of concern for us. On some occasions we may dream of painful or sad situations that seem so real and emotional that we wake up angry or crying. We may also find ourselves waking to find no trace of tears and wonder why. As mentioned, our minds are powerful allies and although our dreams may seem disturbing they can help us to better understand ourselves and gain more awareness. Dreams are often a message from our subconscious in the form of symbols, to tell us something we need to hear or to know about.

Although the first stages of awareness can be somewhat overwhelming, we need to remind ourselves that it is possible to work through these issues and heal from them so that they will no longer have so much power over us and our relationships. If we are beginning to feel, this is because we are ready. We may find it encouraging to trust a higher power to help us through and to provide us with what we need to release and heal!

As we become aware that our emotions are surfacing, we may help ourselves to feel them by focusing on the area of our body that seems to hold the depth of the emotions. If we wish to release our pain we can help to get in touch with it if we focus on the part of our body that represents our emotional center. When we are in touch with grief we usually feel tension in the chest and throat. When we get in touch with deep pain and release it, we may feel a connection with a deep aspect of our own personality located in the region of the heart or in the chest cavity. This can be considered one of the chakras or energy centers that are discussed in many Eastern religions and meditation philosophies. Emotions manifest themselves in various areas of the body and the best way to become aware of them is to learn to be aware of what is going on in the body.

Beginning to Feel Again

Beginning to feel again involves a number of steps and concepts for us to grasp. First, it is simply not possible to flick a switch and begin to feel again. We cannot simply begin to experience feelings generated in the present. When re-establishing our emotions we usually must face the past emotions that we have not dealt with. In other words, we cannot ignore the past when it comes to beginning to feel again.

If we were able to flick a mental switch and turn on our feelings to the full level, we would probably be overwhelmed and not know what to do. Fortunately, our minds are smart enough to recognize when we can or cannot handle the emotions. Our mind will protect us from what we are not yet ready to deal with and therefore protect us from harm.

When we begin to feel again we start a gradual process. Our minds will allow us to feel what we are ready to feel. The mind will have its own agenda and as a result we must be content with getting in touch with feelings as they arise. At times I have heard of therapists or individuals attempting to schedule a time to feel their emotions.

Judging from what I have experienced and what others have expressed to me, suppressed emotions will come to the forefront when we are ready. They are usually triggered by some event such as a scene in a movie, recalling a past event that we had forgotten or events that occur in our dreams. Often our dreams can have a high emotional content, and when going through a catharsis it is not uncommon to wake up from a dream sobbing.

Many people in recovery have expressed that getting in touch with our emotions is similar to peeling an onion. Getting in touch with our feelings involves peeling away one layer at a time. We peel away a layer to find another. Eventually we get down to the core of the onion or the core of our emotions. By this time we usually have a greater understanding of ourselves and have achieved a greater sense of emotional health.

Admitting we are numb and that we are hurting is a major and crucial step in our recovery. Beginning to feel again requires surrendering and accepting that we are hurting. Even though we may not be feeling all the pain and may not be in touch with our feelings, we are in touch with the fact that our state of mind is one of unhappiness and stress. We recognize our previous behavior of running from our emotions.

For many of us, admitting we are hurting may seem like defeat or a failure since we have fought so hard and for such a long time to win this emotional battle. As many recovered people can attest, it is really a victory to admit that we are hurting. It is a crucial step in finally recognizing something about ourselves that we may have been denying for a long time. It is a courageous step and one's first victory in achieving emotional health!

At the same time that we surrender our fight against our emotions, we must develop a commitment to release our suppressed emotions and to heal. At first we may be frightened by the prospect of turning on our emotions and releasing them. However, as our work progresses we will experience benefits from releasing our emotions and begin to comprehend the benefits of our work. If we are not committed to releasing our emotions and healing, it will be easy to slip into old patterns again. Sometimes this will occur, but if we are truly committed to our own healing process then, upon the realization that we are repeating old patterns, we will begin to work on establishing new, more healthy ways of resolving our past feelings.

In the recovery process it is important to give ourselves the permission to feel. We must reassure ourselves that allowing the feelings to surface is OK and will actually benefit us. It is like gradually turning on a tap. The water comes out slowly at first, but we have control of the rate of flow. If something touches us or moves us we should let ourselves feel it. If someone compliments us and we feel sadness, allow ourselves to feel it. If something or someone brings out some anger in us, we should allow ourselves to feel the anger and the hurt behind it.

For a long time we have been in the habit of stuffing our feelings down whenever they appear. We must learn to feel the feelings and let the energy dissipate. We do this by giving ourselves permission to feel, and by allowing ourselves the time and focus to get in touch with what is coming up for us. Allow yourself to feel and be present.

At all times it is also very important to accept whatever we are feeling, be it anger, sadness, joy, or any emotion whether it seems appropriate or not. We may have felt shame for feeling certain ways in the past, or have been ridiculed for crying when young. In some cases expressing joy may also have been considered inappropriate. In some families, numbness and avoidance of expression extends from anger to sadness, to happiness and to joy as well. It is important that we are not judgmental of our emotional states.

It is equally important not to try to rationalize our feelings. If we are feeling a certain emotion or combination of emotions it is OK - even if we cannot explain why we are feeling a certain way. Trying to understand or rationalize why we are feeling a certain way usually gets in the way of being in touch with our feelings and expressing them. Feelings are not meant to be explained. They exist - sometimes illogically. Feelings are feelings. They exist on their own without rationalizations. They just are.

When unresolved emotions surface, we may not know exactly why they are surfacing or what event in our lives caused the original feelings. It is a myth that when we get in touch with some unresolved feeling, our memory of the event will arise at the same time. This may occur, but it is not always the case. Upon further release, however, we may find ourselves remembering things we had long forgotten. The important thing to keep in mind is that the feelings are there and need to be released, regardless of whether we know what caused them in the first place. Many times I went through periods of release not knowing why I was experiencing the feelings I was having at the time. Even without knowing their source, I worked on releasing these feelings. I successfully resolved them and moved myself closer to emotional health.

The Emotion Life Cycle

Earlier in this book a model of emotions was presented. This model included the idea that emotions are processes of energy. The idea of emotional processes can be further enhanced by the idea that an emotion has a natural life cycle of energy that, if fully expressed, results in the dissipation of the emotional energy. Emotions, if allowed to take their course, will come and go on their own. The reality about an emotion is that if it is acknowledged and expressed, then its energy will fade over time unless it is re-stimulated. The problem that most of us experience is that we block the emotional process at one of the four steps in its life or energy cycle.

The first step that brings about emotion is the event itself. The event may bring about sadness or joy or perhaps one of the many other emotions. To start the emotional process we need to acknowledge that the event occurred. This means letting go of the denial process we may have maintained. If we have a habit of denying that we have been hurt or do not give much weight to the positive things that happen in our lives, then we shut the emotional process down at that point. Our bodies may, however, react by moving into a subtle state of awareness involving increased muscle tension and other symptoms. Denying the actual event can often lead to a state of disassociation from reality to a point at which we may not remember certain events. With patients who have experienced Post Traumatic Stress Disorder, symptoms of psychogenic amnesia are quite common.

The next stage that we would normally move into is one of awareness of a feeling. Again, feelings are a whole body/mind experience so the emotion may be experienced in any part of the body as a gut feeling, muscle tension or facial expression. With the body experience also comes a conscious tone to the emotion such as a change in our mood. Again, if the emotional experience is acknowledged and allowed to flow freely, then the stage of expression can occur. Should we try to avoid the awareness by altering our state or using some of the avoidance techniques mentioned earlier, we will likely end up with physical symptoms or a reduction in our ability to think rationally. As mentioned earlier, we will become more sensitive to similar issues and be less willing to tolerate emotional expression in others.

The expression stage can take many forms depending on personal preferences and methods of expressing oneself. In this stage there is no one way of expressing an emotion, and no right or perfect way either. Emotional expression is deeply personal and is really an expression of ourselves. A few techniques and methods of emotional expression, outlined in a later chapter, may help you to discover your own personal style of expression. Again, many people stop the emotional cycle by shutting down and "swallowing" their emotion. Tears are blocked, anger is pushed down and even joy is restrained due to being self-conscious. All of these actions lead to the same symptoms of emotional blocking listed in the previous step. In this step however, since we have awareness, we are doing a greater deal of harm to our self esteem because we are denying our own emotional existence. Nathaniel Brandon wrote that denying our emotions is one of the main causes of low self-esteem. When we deny an emotion we end up committing a crime against our own soul by disowning ourselves.

In the early stages of recovery, an emotional catharsis may leave us with a great deal of energy or alternately we may feel exhausted. The energy that we may experience is like an unconstrained spring. Think of a spring that has been compressed. It is being held down just as our emotions were. Release the spring and the energy in the spring causes it to stretch and recoil until it reaches its natural position. A release of emotions can have the same effect on us. We may experience variations in energy and mood fluctuations in a manner similar to the spring being released.

At this time we may feel exhilaration as the energy we have been using for suppressing is made available to us for other purposes. We may find ourselves requiring less sleep. We may want to change things in our lives. We may seem to be on an emotional roller coaster at times. As we progress through our healing process the amplitude of the waves usually decreases. We will eventually find ourselves in a more normal state where our mood varies to certain degrees but not as widely as in our early stages of healing.

I believe that it is at this time in the healing process, when variations in mood occur, that many people get labeled as manic depressive. Manics are people who have a depressive disorder, and experience wide mood swings. Unfortunately many people consider such a diagnosis a sign of a condition that will last their entire lifetime. While a person who has experienced a substantial loss may experience mood swings, it is important to note that in the process of releasing pent up energy the mood swings may in fact be a natural process of beginning to recognize and deal with one's emotions. As the emotions are expressed, the mood swings should decrease over time.

Returning to a more natural state may take some time. We will discover a new baseline for our consciousness. Until we settle down to our new emotional state, it is better to put off any major decisions or lifestyle changes until we come to terms with our release and gain an understanding of how we feel after the catharsis. Releasing emotion is very demanding and requires energy. Although we may not exert ourselves physically, emotional expression can leave us exhausted. The healing process can take a great deal of energy from our bodies. We may have little or no energy for a period following a release. I often found that a day or two of rest was very helpful. I would find a place to relax, do some reading or curl up with my pet. This period was a time for rejuvenation and consolidation. Go to a park, read a book or watch the children play. Allow your mind's wounds to heal!

A New Emotional Baseline

Completely releasing an emotion may be frightening for some of us simply because we may have never done this before. We may have never experienced the release associated with grieving a loss and healing. A scar will always remain but the wound can heal. We may also be so used to having the emotion that releasing and letting go of it will bring about a sense of unfamiliarity. Even though the emotion does not serve us, it has always been around. To let go of it opens up new possibilities and awareness. We may find ourselves wondering who we really are without all of our emotional baggage.

When we have a depression that has been with us a long time we may actually feel somewhat uncomfortable with it gone. We may have to establish a new emotional baseline for ourselves. Although this may seem somewhat frightening to us, the long term benefits are what we need to focus on. Releasing our unresolved emotions places us in a state of transition. When the pain is gone, we can be more open. Others may feel more open and communicative with us, which may be unfamiliar to us. In addition, we will have given up a part of us that was around for so long. Our depression may have actually seemed to be one of the only consistent things in our lives, although not a very positive one.

By releasing our deep rooted feelings we may find ourselves adjusting to a state of consciousness that seems unfamiliar to us. Part of the depression may have lifted and we begin to feel differently about ourselves and somewhat unfamiliar with our new level of consciousness. At this time we can reduce our fear and insecurity by reminding ourselves that we are in a state of transition and a new beginning. Our lives and emotions will eventually settle, leaving us healed and better prepared to solve problems and feel joy in our lives.

If we have released a great deal of emotion, we may have finally expressed something that we have carried around for ages. The expression and resolution of these long-held feelings has been a subtle part of our consciousness. With these subtle background feelings now resolved and gone, our consciousness can feel different and unfamiliar to us. We may even feel as though we have amputated a part of our consciousness and that our sense of self feels different. We may need to get to know ourselves without our depression or anger. If we have become accustomed to depression, feelings of joy may be unfamiliar to us.

Identifying the Feelings

Present Safety

For many of us, facing our feelings is frightening even though we may realize that it is necessary for our recovery. In our goal of expression and recovery, we can learn to face the feelings with a new sense of discovering new perspectives and new options. We can also discover that, although the pain is being felt in the present, the incident that caused the pain is in the past and that we are removed from it and can experience safety. This sense of safety was not available to us at the time of the hurt.

Body Awareness

One of the best ways to get in touch with an emotion is to relax ourselves and take note of where in our body we are experiencing the feeling and tension. Taking a deep breath will allow us to relax and become more aware of the tension in our body. Are we feeling a sensation in our stomach, neck, shoulders, back, or face? Are our facial muscles tight? Do we feel relaxed? Do we feel an urge to do something or to work on something? By spending some time with ourselves and focusing on our body sensations, we can begin an almost meditative process of unlocking our emotions. Only by slowing down and becoming aware of our body sensations, do we begin to connect with our emotions.

Awareness through Breath

Almost all forms of meditation use breathing as a technique of relaxation or awareness of self. In our emotional work, we can use breathing as a tool of emotional discovery. In *The Mirror of the Body*, authors Kaye and Matchan describe breathing as follows. "There are two kinds of breathing: The automatic, unconscious breathing performed by all living organisms, and the conscious, controlled breathing we can choose to do for a specific purpose." The second type of breathing can be use for two purposes as well. Conscious breathing can be used to induce relaxation or it can be used to increase awareness and aid in the release of emotional tension.

Besides exchanging oxygen and carbon dioxide, breathing also induces a reflex action that nourishes the body. Breathing, which is intricately connected with our nervous system, can be used as a tool in meditation to bring in energy and to remove and release negativity and tension.

Since emotional or nervous tension usually result in a greater degree of muscular tension, the flow of energy and breathing is often restricted. Breathing, although done without any real effort on our part, involves a process of contracting and releasing a great number of muscles. Shallow breathing may be the result of the emotional tension. Taking deep, abdominal breaths can almost always induce an instantaneous sense of relaxation. Accordingly, abdominal breathing can induce changes in brain wave patterns, resulting in a more relaxed Alpha state. Breathing balances, relaxes and restores the body and mind. As Thomas Gaines states in his book *Vitalic Breathing*, "... the act of breathing spreads the life-force through the body."

Knowing that the breath is a source of vitality, we can also identify the breath as a source of focusing and centering ourselves. By relaxing through breath work, we can begin to relieve the tension and become more aware of emotions causing the tension.

Stop, Look, Listen

Often our attempt at identifying feelings can be confusing. Our feelings may not have a name to them. We may also be feeling a combination of feelings at once. Some theorists suggest that there are only four basic emotions - fear, anger, sadness and joy, and that all other emotions are a combination of these four. Perhaps this is possible, however many of the feelings we experience have a subtleness to them that makes their identification more difficult. From the list presented later in this chapter, it can be easier to identify with a more specifically named emotion than with one of the basic four.

The skill of being able to name our feelings is something that we may need to develop. With practice and awareness of what various feelings are like, we can learn to more readily identify the emotions we are experiencing. Having a clearer idea of the feelings we are experiencing can assist us in then identifying the underlying beliefs and memories.

In attempting to be aware of our feelings, we can use the analogy of the sign at a railroad crossing. In the rural areas near where I grew up, there were train crossings without the barriers that would stop traffic if a train was approaching. Drivers were expected to stop before the tracks and use their own judgment as to whether it was safe to cross. These tracks were usually marked with a sign that said "Stop, Look, Listen" These same words can be used as a process of identifying our own feelings.

The first instruction is to stop. This may mean taking some time to put aside what we are doing or to remove our distractions. To stop what we are doing means to suspend our thoughts and to focus on ourselves for a moment. It only takes a few seconds to do this anytime or anywhere. We can do it in the silence of a conversation or between responses. Quite often the focus of counseling is to assist the client in stopping to look inside.

The next step is to look at what is going on in oneself. This may mean focusing in on a vague unfelt sense of tension or anxiety in the body, a sense of lightness in the case of joy, or heaviness in the case of sadness or grief. While we may not be able to identify the emotion at first, we can identify that we are feeling something. At this time, simply listen to your body nonjudgmentally and accept that clarity may come later. In the case of repressed memories there may not be an understanding of why the emotions are occurring. Perhaps there will be no words attached to the feelings.

The third key word of the sign is to listen. Slow down, look inside, notice tension and listen to what sensations we are experiencing. We may be experiencing a combination of feelings. That is OK. Be willing to accept some discomfort and feel what is present. Give the emotions space and room to be present. This will help in the processing of the emotions and subsequent memory recall or increased awareness. Just as a doctor becomes quiet and uses a stethoscope to listen to a patient's heart, so too must we quiet the things around us, focus and listen to what is going on inside us. Doing this allows us to obtain the information we need to gain the awareness required to create a shift in our feelings, behaviors and thoughts.

So, What Am I Feeling?

If someone were to ask you "How are you feeling?" how would you answer? For many of us it may be difficult to accurately answer this question. In some cases we may never have actually been asked such a question. In a society where relationships are built upon communicating, the absence of an understanding of how we are feeling limits our ability to develop close relationships. How can we interact if we are unaware of our feelings? It is difficult to have self knowledge if we are not in touch with our emotions.

So how do you feel? Here's a checklist to help identify emotions. Take a look at this list often; do a self check; try to evaluate which emotions are present and which are not at a given moment. Which emotions have you experienced recently? Which emotions would you like to experience more often?

How am I feeling?

Afraid	Aggressive	Agonized
Angry	Annoyed	Anxious
Apologetic	Arrogant	Bad
Bashful	Bewildered	Blissful
Bored	Cautious	Cheerful
Cold	Contented	Confident
Confused	Content	Curious
Defensive	Demure	Depressed
Detached	Determined	Disappointed
Disapproving	Discouraged	Disbelieving
Disgusted	Disillusioned	Disoriented
Doubtful	Ecstatic	Elated
Embarrassed	Empty	Enraged
Envious	Exasperated	Excited
Exhausted	Exuberant	Fearful
Frenzied	Frightened	Frustrated

Furious	Great	Grief
Guilty	Happy	Hassled
Helpless	Helpful	Hopeful
Hopeless	Horrified	Humbled
Hurt	Hysterical	Indifferent
Innocent	Insecure	Interested
Irritable	Irritated	Isolated
Jealous	Joyous	Liberated
Liked	Lonely	Loving
Mad	Meditative	Mischievous
Miserable	Morbid	Motivated
Negative	Numb	Obstinate
Offended	Optimistic	Outraged
Painful	Panicked	Paranoid
Pessimistic	Perplexed	Powerful
Powerless	Puzzled	Regretful
Relaxed	Relieved	Resentful
Restless	Sad	Satisfied
Scared	Sheepish	Shocked
Skeptical	Smug	Surprised
Sympathetic	Tender	Tense
Thoughtful	Undecided	Uneasy
Unhappy	Unsure	Uptight
Valuable	Vulnerable	Withdrawn
Worthless	Worried	

From the list above, check which ones you are feeling at this moment. Go through each word one at a time and think of a time when the word describes how you once felt. Take the time to also imagine how each word makes you feel and how that word would feel in your body. Remember too, that sometimes we may have no words to describe how we feel. An emotion may be simply a felt sense in our body.

The Healing Process

Although we have built a strong case for emotional expression, it is a fact that emotional expression by itself is not enough to bring about healing. In our earlier model we noted that it was the combination of expression and symbolizations that cause habitual patterns. If we are to resolve those patterns and heal emotionally, we need to examine our attitudes, behavior and self talk as well as express ourselves emotionally. Healing cannot occur unless we work simultaneously on our behavior, emotions and thinking. Fortunately, the three are intricately related and therefore working on one will have positive effects on the others. Too often one of the three will be compromised due to the stress we are experiencing. Just as a drinking habit may numb our emotions and negative thoughts will affect our moods, so too will positive thoughts and emotional expression lead to improved behaviors.

When we are hurting, our thinking tends to shut down as we remember or re-experience the original hurt. As humans, we take pride in our ability to think - but even more important is our ability not to think. By quietening our mind and silencing our thoughts we can connect with our emotive center and listen to our emotions. Doing so often involves recalling a time when we were hurt. This may unconsciously occur when we experience a similar hurt in the present. Our patterns of behavior often result in the re-enactment of situations in which we were hurt before.

Discovering and Unlocking Emotions and Beliefs

When examining an old hurt, it is as if that time and place in which we were hurt, is in the present. Although we may be physically removed from the time and place, when recalling the hurt we are mentally and emotionally at the same time and place of the past event. This is why it is painful to face our emotions. The fear of being hurt can be so strong as to cause us to avoid recalling the feelings of the situation.

In *Therapy for Adults Molested as Children - Beyond Survival,* John Briere writes: "Most papers and texts on the treatment of PTSD (Post Traumatic Stress Disorder) emphasize the need for adequate emotional discharge." Briere states that this emotional discharge is needed regardless of the type of trauma. Even though trauma often results in a tendency to avoid feelings that are similar to the event, facing the emotions and releasing is necessary for recovery.

Recalling the event in present safety and with new insight and awareness, allows us to discharge the emotion in a manner that achieves resolution of the hurt. If we simply recall the event and feel the emotion without the change in symbolization and self talk, then we only re-stimulate the hurt and healing does not occur.

Often the fear of loss of control is heard by therapists and friends. Many people fear that if they start to cry, they'll cry forever. The idea is to relive the original incident in a situation that feels safe for the person, and to ensure that the person knows the pain can be escaped if it becomes unbearable. Often we have become skilled at using our intellect to avoid pain and we can use these skills at such times to our advantage if the pain is overwhelming. It is important to balance the pain of the original incident with the present sense of safety in re-examining the emotions and to emphasize that the person experiencing the pain can return to "present time". This can be accomplished by focusing on objects around the room or by answering various non-emotionally stimulating questions relating to the individual's present situation or daily life.

To resolve pain we need to become our own observer and participant in our pain. In present safety we can experiencing the original pain, fear and threat to ourselves and begin to understand its true nature. T.J. Scheff writes that "When the balance of attention is achieved, the client is both participant in, and observer of, his own distress. Under these conditions, the repressed emotion ceases to be too overwhelming to countenance; the client becomes sufficiently aware of it to feel it and to discharge it." When re-experiencing a hurt, one will feel the pain, fear and danger of the original incident. One must remind oneself that although the experience from the past is very real, the present is safe, and he or she is physically removed from the original danger.

In identifying the beliefs that are trapped in the emotional content, it is also necessary to identify the internal conflict that is causing the anxiety. Usually the conflict is a result of two partially opposing aspects or beliefs. According to Gestalt therapy, resolving the conflict involves the softening of the self towards the unaccepted belief. This does not mean that we accept the behavior of others, but that we become willing to look at the issues that are troubling us. It is a willingness to look inside and to allow the feelings to be part of us and to be acknowledged.

When we do this, a point of balance is maintained and we become as much of an observer as a participant, otherwise a re-stimulation occurs rather than a cathartic experience. By being our own observer, we can become more aware of the true nature of the event, our self talk, and beliefs that we hold about the event. We can then objectively examine the content and nature of the beliefs and whether they are in fact true. With present safety, the assistance of a counselor or a support group and our own improved judgment and self-value, we can better judge if these attitudes, beliefs, self-talk, and messages that we were given were rational.

More often than not, we discover irrationality or improperly laid guilt or responsibility. In other instances we may discover that we made a promise to never be hurt again, never be poor again, or never be ridiculed. Through the discovery of the underlying cause of our pain we can learn to practice acceptance of ourselves and others. We learn that we did the best we could at the time. We can then adjust our attitudes and beliefs accordingly. Learning theorists agree that it is easier to replace a negative habit or belief than to try to eliminate it. From this comes the acceptance that it is easier to change ourselves by substituting a positive belief.

If we believed that we were unworthy and then learned otherwise, if we believed we were bad or brought on the hurt and then realized otherwise, at such moments we discharge and heal. We learn that, now, there is a contradiction between the original situation and the truth of the situation. Our newer, healthier belief contradicts our previous belief, causing us to discharge with a new belief about the situation and ourselves that allows us to heal emotionally.

The content and nature of some of these new beliefs and attitudes are numerous. Here are a few examples:

- we learn that we are now safe.
- we learn that we have power and can do things differently
- we discover that we didn't deserve the treatment we received
- we learn that we were and are lovable
- we discover that we can now make other choices
- we learn that we can remove ourselves from the situation if it were to re-occur
- we learn that we are competent
- we recognize that we were in a no-win situation
- we learn that we are capable of having a happy life
- we learn that we weren't responsible for what happened
- we learn that what happened wasn't fair
- we can see the situation in a different light and perspective
- we can accept that others make mistakes
- we had expectations that weren't met
- we can accept that we did the best we could with our knowledge at the time

When examining and evaluating our beliefs, we must do so without judgment and self-criticism of ourselves. We need to inventory our actions and feelings in a moral and honest manner. We need to look at the values and beliefs we hold in the situation and determine if those values are appropriate. Often we have wholly swallowed the values of the role models around us. In particular, this happens in childhood, when we have yet to develop our own distinct identity, values and belief systems. Later in life we need to examine these beliefs to determine their validity in our own life and the way the world works. We need to evaluate the values, messages, beliefs, self talk, shoulds, level of responsibility, and perhaps how much power we did or didn't have at the time.

The Role of Thinking in Healing

In our healing process it is often necessary to challenge our beliefs about certain events. Often we need to re-evaluate these events and experience a process of learning regarding these events. Although these events were in the past, the emotions associated with them are being felt in the present. While we are focusing on those feelings in the present, we may also need to focus on our current thinking patterns and belief system.

Although we may have established beliefs and patterns, we as humans are intelligent enough to learn and develop new beliefs once we receive new information or insight. Often, the discharge of emotion will result in a greater clarity of thinking that will allow us to examine our belief systems and behaviors.

Some beliefs we hold may not even be apparent to us, simply because they are inferred rather than explicitly expressed. Often well meaning parents will make statements such as "if you do not do well at x, then you will never be or have y." X could represent school, homework, table manners, being quiet, or any other behavior that they want from us. Y could represent any result that they wish, such as going on to college, having friends, a successful marriage, or job. What "Y" represents is their model of success which, in all likelihood, will be accepted as our measure of success, perhaps unconsciously, as something we should obtain.

Statements made to us in such a manner result in an implied "should". For example, my father often scolded me as a child and teenager by telling me that if I did not stop a particular behavior that was annoying to him, I would lose all my friends. A statement such as this says a number of things. I felt that I had been told that my friends did not value other qualities in me and would give up on me simply because of one or two minor weaknesses. In addition, there were other messages that I internalized from these parental behaviors. What I recently realized is that I had internalized the idea I should always have a number of friends, and that if I did not have a number of friends, then I was unsuccessful. This placed an unconscious burden on myself to satisfy this implied should. By coming to recognize this implied belief, I was able to resolve these feelings and feel a greater sense of self acceptance and comfort with being alone with myself.

My realization, that I described above, is a cognitive realization. These realizations are just as important to our healing process as is emotional expression. These changes in our cognition or thinking lead to changes in our emotional state. Changes in behavior can also have similar impact on our emotional state. To change our behavior, we often need to gain an understanding of our moods. This involves measurement and diagnosis of our moods. In *The Feeling Good Handbook*, Dr. David Burns outlines a process of measurement and diagnosis of moods, and identifies distortions in thinking. He then provides practical solutions involving the modification of our thinking for these problem areas.

Another important aspect of healing is the linking of insights with feelings. Insights are essentially useless if they are without attachment to our feelings. If the insights are purely intellectual then they have no effect on our emotions. It is through the combination of insight and feelings that we achieve healing and growth.

Altogether, healing involves developing a new cognitive map of ourselves and of the world in which we live. It involves challenging our cognition, our behavior and our emotions. We may learn a great deal about human nature, about ourselves and about others. We may discover new aspects of ourselves, new creativity and new talents. We will grow in understanding and self knowledge.

In earlier years there may have been a time when we thought that the pain would never end. As a child we may not have the ability, simply due to our age or circumstances, to reach out to someone or to find a safe place from our troubles. At times as an adult we may not have had the tools, support, help, or knowledge to reach out and go through the healing process. The pain may have seemed endless.

As adults we can make choices and we can find help. There are numerous 12-step groups (such as Al-Anon, Adult Children Anonymous, Alcoholics Anonymous or Emotions Anonymous) that can provide support and help in your healing process. There are counselors trained to help and guide you through this process. Keep in mind also that, although you may feel as though you are the only one with this problem, there are others who have experienced similar problems, have healed and are willing to help. Go to a 12-step group and see for yourself. We can learn that emotional pain can be resolved and that we can find joy - even if it is for the first time!

Resolving Results in New Behavior

As noted in the model, our emotional stages follow from an event to reactivity, to symbolization and lead to habitual patterns. These habitual patterns then filter through to our consciousness. Often we try to resolve a behavior pattern by developing new habits and by trying to counteract the behavior itself. In terms of our emotional-behavioral model, this involves working downward from consciousness to affect the habitual pattern.

A more appropriate and likely more effective method to alleviate the behavior pattern would be to go to the root or foundation of the problem by re-examining the event, emotional expression and symbolizations that result in the pattern. This type of self examination will bring about a longer lasting solution to the problem than the short term attempts at changing habits to bring about behavior modification. Both methods will cause change in behavior, but examining the root issues will bring about a resolution of the emotional distress and more lasting result.

Since a surprising proportion of our behavior can be the result of emotional distress, alleviating the emotion can result in the removal of the distressful behavior. Once the emotional distress is dealt with, we no longer have to resort to obsessive or compulsive behavior in an attempt to block the emotions. We may no longer need to reach for a drink, drug or other addictive substance to escape from our pain. We may begin to experience closeness as we become more open and genuine. We can take off our emotional masks without fear. We will also likely have a greater capacity for rational thinking once we release and resolve our emotional distress. Habitual patterns of behavior that were a symptom of our distress are removed from our daily lives because we have resolved the deeper problem.

Since emotions affect, our behavior, the question should be asked "do behaviors affect our emotions?" Clearly they do. Current research has indicated that certain behaviors increase the level of serotonin in the brain. Since depressed people tend to have lowered serotonin levels, certain behaviors can help alleviate depression. In *The Healthy Pleasures*, authors Robert Ornstein Ph.D. and David Sobel M.D. describe a number of pleasures that are within our reach everyday that can add to our enjoyment and fulfillment. These pleasures may involve such things as investing in yourself, developing a pursuit of happiness, telling yourself a good story, and developing healthy pleasure points. Other behaviors such as meditation, art therapy, and singing have been known to reduce levels of depression.

Often the expression of emotion leads to new behaviors, and new behaviors lead to better emotional states as well as more rational thinking. All three are linked together. Changing one affects the other, which in turn produces other changes. Pick the easier things to change, and you'll notice results!

A recent study in California has shown that changes in behavior and cognitive therapy can bring about changes in the chemicals in the brain, including the structure that is implicated in Obsessive Compulsive Disorder.

In the process of studying the cognitive-behavioral model of counseling theories, therapists-to-be learn that this theory proposes that if we control what we are thinking and doing, then the feelings and physiology will follow. The analogy used is that of a car: the thinking and doing are the front wheels that steer the car, while the feelings and physiology follow right behind.

While these concepts are valid, it is important to note that feelings of sadness and depression can come from more than one source. Feelings of sadness and depression can be generated from our own thoughts and behavior. A negative attitude will lead us to depression. Behavior that isolates us can also lead us to depression.

But another source of sadness and depression occurs when we are emotionally hurt or experience a loss. These feelings are not the result of our thinking or doing, but a natural reaction to a life event. The process of grieving needs to be completed to resolve these feelings. Emotional expression may be required to resolve feelings of sadness, anger or resentment concerning a loss or trauma.

In treating depression and emotional hurt it is necessary to recognize that there are two different sources of emotional pain, both requiring different treatments. In cases of trauma, it may be necessary to re-examine and mentally revisit the incident to resolve the feelings. Simply trying to feel better by changing our thinking may work for some but not all.

If, however, we combine emotional expression and changing our thinking and behavior, then the results can often be astounding in terms of healing, growth and personal development.

Getting Un-Stuck

No problem can be solved from the same consciousness that created it.   -Albert Einstein

In our healing journey there will often be times when we get stuck. In these times we do not see solutions and we seem to repeat patterns of behavior. Sometimes a lesson or test reappears, yet we make the same mistakes or simply don't know what to do. At times it may be our own behavior or attitudes that get us stuck. We fall into a trap or hole. To become unstuck means to learn to recognize the holes we fall into and to acknowledge them and eventually learn to walk around them. Some of these holes and traps are:

fear	helplessness	guilt
despair	powerlessness	fear of failure
isolation	loss of control	panic

Often these feelings or states arise because we do not understand what our body is telling us about our feelings. We may lack knowledge or feel overwhelmed by the signals. Often, as well, we may fear being wrong or being rejected for showing our emotions. We may also be playing old tapes of a past situation in which we may have been helpless or powerless. Again, we need to achieve a sense of balance that tells us that in the present we do have choices and that we can act differently than we have in the past.

We need to recognize that we have options and that we are no longer powerless or helpless. When we recognize these qualities of our new present situation, our fear and despair disappear. We can learn that discharge and healing can bring an end to the isolation that occurs when emotions are accumulated. Remember that crying due to the pain of hopelessness and despair is different from crying for the purpose of healing.

The Self Pity Trap

Often when we are sad or grieving it is easy to fall into a trap of self pity. Self pity involves feeling overly sad for ourselves as victims. If we are finding ourselves developing a "poor me" attitude, then we may need to look into our pattern of being helpless and without power. In our emotional healing we need to remember that we are not helpless and that we can change our situation. Our goal is to heal and be free of lingering sadness rather than remain a slave to it. We need to realize that we are much more than the pain we carry around and that we are much more than our emotional state. Although we may have carried our pain around for a long time, we need to entertain the idea that it is possible to rise out from it and to experience a more joyful state of being. Our emotional state is not necessarily part of our personality. It is something that can be resolved and released to reveal a more creative and energetic self.

Self pity does have its value in our healing process. Identifying that we are feeling pity for ourselves can help us discover that there is some hurt to be resolved or simply that we need to acknowledge that we are feeling sad or unhappy about something. To deny the sadness is to deny our feelings, but to remain in the pity can be a trap that will block our emotional healing. True, it is part of healing to feel sorry for ourselves as this can be a natural part of the healing process, but when this becomes an excuse for the way we are, then we are not healing but hiding. We are avoiding going further along in our healing process.

Imagine a triangle with feeling, pity, and denial each in a corner. In our healing process we may move from corner to corner of the triangle, however our most healing times can occur when we are operating at the center of the triangle. Denial plays its role in healing by allowing us to deal only with what we can handle. Overwhelming ourselves can be harmful and can place a great deal of stress on our mind and body. Pity and sadness allow our mind to acknowledge our sadness and that we have been hurt, but we must eventually move closer to the center position of detachment.

Detachment is a term often used in 12-step groups that

describes a sense of objectivity from others and our problems. Detachment means that we can objectively see the problem in its true light, without the clouds of emotional patterns that have sabotaged our objective thinking. For example, we may have given our power to others or allowed others to be our unofficial parents. As a result we end up reliving our roles with our parents with these people, thus clouding our undestanding of our needs and desires of these people.

Detachment also means being able to the differentiate our problems from other people's problems. Through detachment we learn not to suffer from the reactions and actions of other people. We begin to develop our sense of self esteem measured by our own set of judgments and values as well as a strong belief in our selves. We learn to accept that it is not possible to have everyone like us. By developing a sense of balance between feeling, self-pity, and denial, we can learn about ourselves, acknowledge our own feelings, and see issues in a realistic and objective manner.

Holding On

Many of us unsuspectingly become stuck in the last stage of emotional release. Many of us get to the expression stage and genuinely work on expressing ourselves. To complete the process we need to be willing to let go of the emotional energy. We need to be willing to exist with the issue at hand being completed and gone from our lives. Sometimes a particular emotion has been around us so long that it feels as though it is part of us. To let it go may mean rediscovering ourselves and finding out who we might be, without the emotion that has defined our behavior for such a long time. We may not be happy with the emotions we are experiencing but we may feel comfortable having them around. They become a possession that we are unwilling to part with.

Too often we refer to anger or other emotions with the word "my" in front of it. We end up claiming ownership of our anger. Instead of saying this anger, we say my anger or my sadness. We end up holding it close to our chest and are afraid of letting it completely go. Letting go of an emotion means risk. It means that we will be moving on to the next issue in our lives. This may frighten us to some degree and as a result we cling to our current emotional state. The cost of not going all the way with our emotional expression is that we hang on to the emotion and it can then be easily re-stimulated. Imagine trying to launch a toy boat in a pond with a small string attached to it and tied to the shore. The boat will head off but it will never be able to sail freely or continue on its journey. Emotions are the same in that we must be willing to completely let go of them, otherwise we end up in a state of emotional tension that never quite fully resolves itself.

In order to successfully release the energy associated with our emotions, we must be willing to go completely through the process of release, to simply become aware of the emotion and feel it is not enough. We need to be able to completely express it, then fully let it go and dissipate. We must be willing to let the emotion leave us. It is especially easy to get in touch with anger or sadness, to feel part of it and then back off.

When we do this we simply re-traumatize ourselves. We trick ourselves into thinking that we are doing well by experiencing the emotions. To achieve emotional health we must go further. We must be willing to completely express the emotion and completely let it go. We must get in touch with the feelings, feel them, express them, and let them leave us. If we hold on to them, then they will stay with us and we will not achieve a release.

Increasing our Awareness

In order to solve our problems it is often helpful to examine and expand our scope and awareness of our problem. Often we become stuck because we fail to see other options. Just as though our problem were confined to a small room, we end up breathing only stale air that surrounds the problem. We need to bring some fresh air in or, as the saying goes, "shed some light" on the problem. This can be achieved by searching for new ideas and expanding our range of solutions. It is possible that we may decide to stop resisting our problem. It takes much more effort to resist something than to actually do something about it.

It is often helpful to step back and look at others who were involved in the original problem. I always felt responsible for an incident that happened walking to school in grade one. Reviewing the incident and remembering who else was there helped identify that there were other more mature people around who could have done something so that things would have turned out differently.

Finding others with a similar problem can also help identify other possible solutions. We may try changing our patterns of behavior or simply decide that we no longer need to be a victim, because being a victim often precludes us from accepting responsibility for ourselves. We can more closely examine the responsibilities and roles that others had in the situation. There may also be an opportunity to look inside and discover what our own feelings and beliefs are and whether these beliefs are rational. Insanity is doing the same thing again and expecting different results. We may also begin to look at our expectations. If we can imagine our problem as being within the context of a larger plan, we may be able to look at it more objectively and seek outside help.

Reaching a Crisis Point

Although it would be nice to think that humans constantly strive to solve their problems on their own initiative, it is often a crisis that precipitates an increase in understanding. I have often joked with friends that many of the lessons I have learned were affectionately called an 'AFGE' — Another Friggin' Growth Experience. It has often been noted in the Alcoholics Anonymous and other 12-step programs, that reaching a crisis point, or 'hitting bottom' is crucial to the clients' recovery and subsequent elimination of the addictive behavior. In the case of career choices, many career decisions are made due to a career crisis such as a loss of job or health. In both these cases clients often later regard the crisis as a positive event that dramatically changed their lives.

A crisis point may result from the building of tension and emotional stress that becomes unbearable due to a financial, relationship, or health crisis. It also may occur as the result of recalling incidents that were long forgotten. It seems that many individuals attempt to ignore a crisis, often leading to behavioral problems and emotional distress.

Since crises often appear to bring about long-term positive change, I believe it is important to recognize that the events that occur in our lives seemingly happen for a purpose — to nudge us along to our next level of understanding.

What is Healing?

The Aspects of Healing

In describing the meaning of healing, it is necessary to examine a number of aspects of one's life. Catharsis alone may bring relief; however, if beliefs are not changed, does healing really occur? Similarly, if we alter our beliefs but persist in unhealthy behaviors, we cannot truly claim that we have completed our healing work. Therefore, a definition of healing is complex. Let's examine the major aspects of healing.

First, healing involves the removal of lingering emotional hurt through resolution of the pain. How we do this may be personal and unique to our own situation, beliefs and circumstances. It involves identifying and processing unresolved events so that the emotional content becomes information and our personal history.

Furthermore, healing involves resolving the "shoulds" and "musts" that we tell ourselves and that others have placed on us. If we are living by someone else's standards and expectations, then we are not truly living our own lives. We need to recognize these expectations, some of which may be only indirectly implied. When we start to live by our own rules of consideration for ourselves and others, we will be able to define what our own expectations are. We will achieve a greater sense of self and self-fulfillment. We need to challenge other people's beliefs that we have swallowed without evaluation. Do we wish to own and maintain a particular belief? We need to integrate the parts of ourselves that we disowned or cut off to please others. Often this was done simply to survive in a threatening environment.

A memory I recalled through healing work was that as a young child, I used to love to dance and sing for my parents. I would run from the living room to the kitchen and dance for them, having queued up my favorite record. One day my mother shouted at me "stop being so ridiculous and silly." I ran back to the living room stifling my tears. From that day on I stopped dancing and the process of shutting down my creativity began. Through my healing work I have re-connected with my singing voice and have joined a choir. I now play guitar and have taken voice lessons, discovering that it is never too late to enjoy the talents I have. Another aspect of my healing process, particularly with my music, involved reducing or removing self criticism and the tendency to be hard on myself.

Healing also involves the acceptance of responsibility for our choices and accepting that we may not have been responsible or deserving of what happened to us. Healing is also about setting boundaries and developing the self respect we deserve but may not have received. Often victims of abuse will feel a sense of shame or guilt. This is often perpetrated by the abuser but over time the victim may internalize these messages. It is necessary to challenge these unfounded beliefs and feelings and learn to consider that we are lovable and did not deserve what occurred. We need to challenge our self talk and respond with more positive and loving messages to ourselves.

As with our self talk, healing involves challenging our behavior and learning new responses. In the case of addictions, we may need to learn how to reach for help or assistance, and to share and express our feelings in new ways, rather than numbing them with our addictive behavior. This can be a frightening prospect, but a rewarding action when we learn that we can manage our feelings in more productive ways.

Healing also involves revisiting old issues, challenges and traumas, and resolving them. It also involves the acceptance and integration of feelings and memories. New feelings may emerge from this process as well as memories long forgotten. Healing may also involve learning to let others help and learning to trust again.

Other behavior changes may be more profound. We may choose to associate with a more positive group of people, to become more assertive, or to diminish certain behaviors. In cases of addictions, we may decide to call someone for support, or go to a 12-step meeting, rather than repeat the addictive behavior.

Instead of repeating a behavior, we try a new behavior. This more often than not brings about new and different results, moving us towards greater emotional maturity and self understanding. By changing our behavior we end up changing our feelings. Conversely, by changing our feelings we end up changing our behavior. Additionally, changing our behavior can change our thinking, and changing our thinking also changes how we feel. In other words, our thinking, feeling and behavior are interrelated. In our healing process it is necessary to work on all three, but a change in one area will often lead to changes in others. It is a complex process that begins with small changes in the way we manage ourselves.

Finding One's Voice

So many of us have, at times, been truly victimized. We did not ask for what we got, and although we tried to change things, we were unsuccessful due to the enormity of the problem. Learned helplessness is a recognized pattern that develops when a person is unable to effect solutions to a problematic situation. For many children, the ability to implement solutions to their problems is hampered and restricted by the behavior of the adults around them. As a result, many adults carry around a belief that they cannot help themselves. They do not recognize that they can find their own voice and personal ability to change some aspects of their lives. People who have been victimized sometimes remain in the role of victims. Some go as far as having a vested interest in being sad and being victimized, thereby becoming the perpetrators of their own unhappiness.

Reclaiming our lives and finding our own voice and autonomy can lead to a more fulfilling life and increased joy and happiness. To do this we need to become more comfortable with our interests and values. Are we fearful of others finding out what kind of books and music we read and listen to? Are we afraid to decorate and put up posters that will show others what we believe in? Perhaps creating your own bookshelf that shows others who you are can be a helpful conversation starter. We can begin to let others know of our talents and interests. We can also become an initiator rather than always waiting around for someone else to start something! Doing so can help us develop a sense of competency.

Developing a Healthy Lifestyle

As mentioned earlier, healing work is not complete unless we put into practice what we have learned. Often this involves separating from an unhealthy life, beginning to experience a healthier life and eventually living a healthy life. What are the aspects of a healthy life? I believe the answer to this question lies in a research project by Dr. Rod McCormick at the University of British Columbia. Dr. McCormick interviewed 50 First Nations adults to identify critical incidents concerning the facilitation of healing. Over 400 incidents were then categorized. I believe these categories, referred to as "healing facilitators", are representative of the aspects of leading a healthy lifestyle and are also actions we can take to move towards a healthy lifestyle.

The categories identified (in random order) were as follows:

1. Establishing a social connection.
2. Anchoring oneself in tradition.
3. Exercise.
4. Self Care.
5. Involvement in challenging activities.
6. Expressing oneself.
7. Obtaining help/support from others.
8. Participation in ceremony.
9. Setting goals.
10. Helping others.
11. Gaining an understanding of the problem.
12. Establishing a spiritual connection.
13. Learning from a role model.
14. Establishing a connection with nature.

In reviewing the list, it is clear that these behaviors and actions are all positive steps that can help establish a positive, healthy lifestyle. In my own experience, I believe it is necessary to maintain a sense of balance and effort in each of the above categories. It is interesting to note that most of the above take place when one is involved in a 12-step program!

Resolving Anger and Resentment

The Nature of Anger

I believe that the term anger is often used incorrectly to describe a range of emotions and states such as resentment, aggression and even rage. While anger can often lead to aggression, it is possible to express anger without aggressive behavior. Rage is a state in which someone is out of control. We can also differentiate anger from resentment. Resentment is a slow burning and self-fed poison that eats away at one's soul. Resentment does considerably more harm to the person doing the resenting.

Of all the emotions, anger seems to be the one that we can easily feed and build upon. Like adding wood to a fire, our thoughts can easily increase the heat and intensity of our anger to the point that we are in a rage. I have always found it important to develop an awareness of when I am feeding my own anger, and to recognize and become more rational and accepting at these times. Instead of working myself up, I recognize my level of anger and ask myself what I need and what I am expecting from the other people in the situation.

Anger, when expressed appropriately, can be an excellent path of communication under certain circumstances. In order for anger to be successfully resolved, the anger must be directed at the appropriate person. If we are angry at Bob and tell John, then although we seem to be expressing our anger, we are in fact venting to a third party with no resolution. If we are angry at Bob then we must communicate with Bob. The other option is to let go of the issue.

In addition, successful resolution of anger usually requires considerate behavior of the person with whom we are angry. If the person we are expressing our anger with does not listen or does not adjust their behavior, then we end up remaining angry and possibly getting angrier. We will also end up with a greater degree of anger if the other person retaliates rather than listens.

Resolving anger often requires that we develop new insights or change our own expectations of the other person or organization. Resolving anger may require that we adjust our own behavior. A further consideration is that our anger may be out of proportion to the actual event due to unresolved issues. Often we transfer anger towards a person when they remind us of someone else with whom we are angry. This type of transference occurs with other feelings as well, but more frequently occurs with anger. In a situation like this, we need to step back and observe our own issues. We need to gain insight as to why we are really angry at this person or if the anger seems unreasonable. We must be careful though, because the concept of anger transference can be used as a defense by someone we are angry with to avoid dealing with the actual issue at hand.

Is Yelling Necessary?

Very few people realize that anger can be released without shouting or yelling. Once we start to yell and shout, the other person becomes defensive and effectively stops listening. Think of a time when someone has yelled at us. Do we listen carefully to each word he or she is saying? No, our listening skills are turned off almost immediately when someone yells at us. Anger expressed in a firm confident tone will usually get the message across much more effectively. When anger is communicated without yelling, the other person will not be as defensive and miss what we are trying to communicate.

By speaking in a firm, confident and self respecting tone we end up emphasizing what we are trying to get across and the other person is more likely to listen. Once voice levels start to rise, the other person usually responds in the same manner until we are in a shouting match in which no one wins. By keeping our voices firm and not matching someone else's yelling we can effectively communicate our thoughts and feelings.

Once we have expressed our anger, we will usually uncover the hurt that created the anger in the first place. This hurt will usually manifest itself as sadness that can be released through acceptance, writing and crying. Remember that anger does not need to be acted on. It only needs to be acknowledged and to have its energy dissipated through healthy methods of expression or changes in our thinking and expectations.

Critical Parent Vs Inner Child Anger

In the last few years a great deal of attention has been focused on inner child work. The concept of the inner child comes from the field of transactional analysis which is founded on the principle that each of us has three separate yet combined aspects of our personality. These three aspects are the parent, adult and child. The parent aspect nurtures the individual, while the adult does the reasoning. It is thought that most of our emotions arise from our inner child.

Anger can be somewhat different in that the anger may come from the child or it may also be the result of our own internal "critical parent". In the case of anger generated by the critical parent, we may be angry due to expectations not being met in ourselves or others. When we get angry with ourselves for letting ourselves down, it may be the critical parent to whom we are listening. At these times we need to be less critical of ourselves and more accepting of our limitations at the time. This will result in less anger towards ourselves.

If the anger comes from the inner child it is usually a result of an unmet need. When we are angry with someone we can often bring about more understanding by replacing any four letter words with "I need". If we can recognize and communicate our needs to others then we are less likely to be let down.

The third center of anger is that of the adult. In situations in which the adult in us judges that we are being improperly treated, anger will result. Under these conditions we need to call attention to other people's behavior and communicate that we do not accept it as appropriate. This type of anger is the most rational of the three but only if our expectations are reasonable.

In understanding our anger we also need to recognize that it is complex. Combinations of child, adult and critical parent anger can occur as we move through the expression of our emotions. When we tolerate someone else's inappropriate behavior, we may bring about adult anger, with a critical parent component criticizing ourselves for putting up with it. At the same time, our inner child may feel that his or her needs have not been met.

Mark Linden O'Meara

Anger as a Secondary Emotion

Anger has also been referred to as a secondary emotion since it often gives way to tears. Anger is a warning to us that some expectation is not being met or that we have been hurt. If we examine the source of this anger and discover the hurt, the anger usually subsides as we recognize the hurt. Care must be taken not to perpetuate a mask of victimization by always reducing our anger to tears. Sometimes we are just plain angry and need to express it, but fear of expressing anger gets in the way. Learning to be more comfortable with our anger and expressing our needs can lead us out of a victim role.

Anger that is repressed can manifest itself in a number of ways. For a long time after the passing of my father, I seemed to have a very negative attitude towards a number of people, including my family. This negative attitude was noticeable by the friends who would tolerate it. There seemed to be no resolution to this negativity until I realized that the negative attitude was a manifestation of my anger. Since at the time I was not comfortable at expressing my anger, it seeped through in other ways. As I found ways to express the energy in my emotions, the negative attitude began to disappear and was replaced by a more positive outlook. In this case, anger was the underlying or secondary cause of the problem I was experiencing.

Changing Our Expectations

It is a fact of life that people often let us down. When this occurs we may feel disappointment, resentment, anger, or a range of other emotions. Although it is reasonable to expect people to keep appointments and promises, we must remember that others, being human, are subject to their own strengths and weaknesses. If we continually place expectations on others then we are likely to be often disappointed and angry. This is especially true if our belief system and expectations do not allow for the occasional failure. To expect means to also accept disappointment in our lives. We cannot change others, but we can change ourselves. We do want to maintain standards in our friendships and relationships, but if our expectations are unreasonable, we are bound to end up angry at times.

An example that comes to mind is the fact that I used to have an unreasonable expectation that friends would be around forever. It is a fact that people grow, and as a result, sometimes we outgrow our friends or our friends outgrow us. Because of my unreasonable expectation and my inability to let go, I found myself constantly fretting and getting angry over the friendships that had faded away. By recognizing the nature of these friendships, and acknowledging that one or both of us had moved on, I was able to change my expectations and therefore reduce and eliminate my anger.

Expressing and Releasing Anger

You will recall that emotions generally have three components: a subjective feeling, muscular-skeletal changes, and physiological changes. In my opinion, the expression of anger in particular requires some form of muscular contraction in its expression and resolution. When we are angry our shoulders, arms and neck tense. It is difficult to be angry without muscular tension.

For some of us though, our anger may only be felt in our internal voice. We may feel our anger in our heads but if we are passive, we may not express ourselves since the release of anger involves muscular action. We may find ourselves angry but without any muscular tone appearing. This indicates a disconnection of our emotional senses from the physical. This may have developed from consistently repressing our anger in an environment in which expressing our anger was unsafe. We can undo this form of training by connecting physically with our anger when we find our internal voice is expressing anger. Begin to sense the energy in your anger by clenching your fists and shoulder muscles and learn to release the energy in healthy ways.

I have also found that a poor night's sleep can result when suppressing anger. I often found myself feeling drained of energy in the morning. Instead of repressing it and falling asleep, I found that feeling the anger and expressing it by journaling or some form of energy release would be more productive and energizing. Upon its release, I would often sleep better.

As mentioned, in learning to release anger, we need to find constructive ways to allow the energy of the anger to flow without the anger turning into aggression. Following are a number of techniques that I have found helpful in the safe, physical expression of anger. Many of these techniques can be enhanced by combining them with journalling or writing to express the thoughts that came to mind. We can also write about any sense of resolution that we experience.

Constructive Expression

Repressing anger can consume a tremendous amount of energy, but it is also possible to tap into and expend this energy in creative endeavors and to complete constructive tasks. I remember a time in university when I was experiencing a great deal of anger. I used the energy to clean, scrub and paint my apartment. At another time I used my anger energy to complete some renovation work. The section of wall to be moved came apart a lot more quickly with this energy!

We can take on a project with the energy that flows from anger. Renovations, and physical work such as chopping wood or cleaning up a back yard are tasks that bring positive results from the anger's energy. The idea is to use the energy to effect a positive change.

Yelling Into A Pillow

An expression method, similar to using primal scream techniques, is to use a pillow to cover our faces as we allow ourselves to scream as a child would when angry. The scream allows us to express a raw form of energy and brings about a release of tension. In reviewing some First Nations' literature on healing practices, I discovered that Native Americans have a healing ritual that involves screaming in the woods to bring about a catharsis. Perhaps the ability to scream and make noise is what attracts some people to spectator sports. In such a crowd setting, our screaming and release is not judged, in fact it is encouraged!

Of course, once outside of the sports facilities, one may worry about neighbors and roommates. If you wish to release through this method, you may want to find an appropriate time and place so you won't be alarming them. If you are concerned about the police showing up, all you have to do is explain to the officers that you are working on some anger issues. They will usually leave you be unless you are disturbing someone. Screaming into the pillow provides some noise proofing and gives a destination for the vocal energy.

Perhaps if each of us had a soundproof place we would be more likely to yell and scream and express our anger. Many of us possess such a place. Today's automobiles are virtually sound proof and will mask any yelling. A passenger seat with a pillow on it also makes a great punching bag. While one should never express emotions while driving, one can find a safe place to park such as a side or country road, where one will not be disturbed. If anyone shows up you can take a few deep breaths and relax and then move to another spot. If a police officer shows up, simply explain what you are doing. If they have a problem with what you are doing, they will tell you to move on.

Wet Towel Wringing

This technique was brought to my attention by a singer whom I met at a folk club. I have also heard about it from a few counselors who assist clients in developing healthy methods of anger release. If you really want to work your shoulder and arm muscles, then the towel wringing technique is a great way to express anger. Take a towel and wet it, then wring the towel as tight as you can, using your anger energy to wring out each and every last drop of water. The amount of energy one can put into wringing a towel is surprising, and as a result this technique is a very effective way to release anger. It seems to work well with a dry towel as well.

While doing this, you may want to concentrate on what you are angry about and allow yourself to wring the towel as tightly as you can. I have often found that this technique resolves a great deal of muscle tension in my shoulders. Sometimes it feels almost as good as a massage!

Physical Exercise

Becoming involved in sports can greatly reduce tension. Even a walk or stretching exercises can help in improving our health. In addition to numerous benefits, exercise has been shown to increase levels of serotonin.

Sports, such as racquetball, that provide indirect competition with another player by bouncing a ball off a wall can be an excellent means of clearing our tension from anger. It is important to ensure that the anger does not turn into inappropriate aggression, otherwise the sport will not be as enjoyable for you or other team members. If it is not possible to make it to the gym, you can go for a brisk walk or bike ride.

Letting Your Inner Child Have a Tantrum

Many of our emotions come from our inner child. Often we can be frustrated by something or down-right angry. Although not appropriate socially or when used for manipulative purposes, a temper tantrum in the privacy of our own home can help release the energy associated with anger. Tantrums are usually short in duration. The physical release of energy through jumping up and down and stomping our feet can help us let off steam. It can help calm us down somewhat.

Squeezing An Image with Fists

A gentler exercise for anger expression is to clench our fists while we imagine that we are holding a miniature of the person we are angry at in each fist. As we clench our fists, we squeeze the person tight and feel the anger in our arms and shoulders. We then release our fists and imagine putting the person down unharmed. This exercise can be helpful in releasing the anger and promoting forgiveness.

Is Forgiveness Necessary?

In our healing process we may ask ourselves whether it is necessary to forgive those who have harmed us. Before answering this question we need to evaluate and clarify our understanding and definition of forgiveness.

First and foremost, forgiveness is something we do for

ourselves. It is an act of restoring sanity to ourselves by changing our own attitudes and feelings. In forgiveness, we do not condone the actions of others, nor do we minimize the impact that those actions had on us. It is not a process of wiping the slate clean. It is a process of acknowledging what occurred, the impact of those actions or events, and the work we have done to cope and resolve the problems. It is not a method of minimizing or denying our pain.

Secondly, forgiveness does not always mean reconciliation. Forgiveness can occur without reconciliation or an apology from the offender. It is also important to note that forgiveness is not something we do only once. It is an ongoing process.

If we do not forgive, then we end up living with resentment and bitterness. By not forgiving, we end up harming ourselves. Terry Waites, upon his release from his hostage ordeal, stated that he had to forgive his captors, otherwise he would remain captive forever.

While moving forward in our healing process we may consider confronting the abuser. In such cases it is extremely important that we understand our expectations regarding the confrontation. It is important to stop further abuse, however additional pain can occur due to our expectations of the abuser. We may expect them to apologize and dramatically change their behavior. Some abusers will deny the abuse. Others may admit to it and apologize, yet continue with abusive behavior due to their own difficulties and problems. Others may begin their own process of recovery, while others may be resentful.

In our quest to forgive we need to give up the notion that the perpetrator owes us something or needs to make up for what they did or did not do. Only when we give up this notion can we have truly forgiven.

While confrontation may be a necessary part of our healing process, so is forgiveness. Healing involves forgiving ourselves as well as others. It is a step that we take to rid ourselves of resentment and bitterness. It can be a difficult and challenging, yet rewarding, process in which we free ourselves of a burden and release others from our expectations.

Methods of Emotional Release and Healing

In the following pages you will find a number of techniques that I have come across that can be used to facilitate emotional expression. One aspect to be stressed at this point is that each person's emotional healing process is personal and unique. In reviewing the techniques below, you may find that some of these will suit you while others may not. Just as the interests of people vary, so do the ways that people express themselves and heal. Keep in mind that there is no right way nor a wrong way to express oneself as long as your method does not harm others.

The Creative Arts and Self Expression

Artistic Expression

Pablo Picasso was quoted as saying that "art washes away the dust of daily living from the soul". Art of any form has been known for ages to have tremendous healing powers when some medium is used to express the feelings and creative center of the artist. In referring to artists, we wish to include all forms of art — dancing, music, painting, sculpting, or any other form of expression. Art therapy has been a very successful treatment for those who are recovering from the trauma of being sexually abused.

In using art as a healing medium of expression, it is important to create art that is expressive. If one places an object on a table and paints it, then the exercise of painting will be relaxing but not as healing as using a canvas or other medium to express one's feelings and emotions.

In times of healing and recovery, many people re-discover a talent they had abandoned. Others may discover a talent that they never knew they had. In many high schools we see a great deal of artistic talent that falls by the wayside upon graduation. Perhaps it may be time to try things you always wanted to or were afraid to do. A key to using the creative arts is to accept whatever you create and avoid judging it as good or bad.

Dance and Drama

Healing through expression is not limited to art alone. Meditation, visualization, singing (a form of meditation in some cultures), chanting, role playing, and dance can all play an important role in the healing process.

In *Creative Therapies in the Treatment of Addictions*, author Lynn Johnston states in her abstract that "the core issue in addiction is shame, and creativity can serve as the antidote to this shame. Creativity may take the form of poetry therapy, art therapy, dance therapy, or musical/dramatic performance."

In another study entitled *Dance Movement: A therapeutic program for psychiatric clients*, author Lou Heber reports that when using dance therapy, patients reported an increase in self-esteem. Fern Leventhal, in *Dance/movement therapy with battered women*, reports that "by motivating female victims of domestic violence to act, dance/movement therapy addresses patterns of helplessness, ambivalence, and inactivity. Dance/movement interventions help women (and men) internalize a positive self-concept as well as gain physical and emotional control."

Musical Expression

Musical expression can also be very helpful in the release of emotional energy. In *Care of the Soul*, Thomas Moore writes "one of my own forms of expression is to play the piano in times of strong emotion. I remember well the day Martin Luther King Jr. was killed. I was so overwhelmed that I went to the piano and played Bach for three hours. The music gave form and voice to my scrambled emotions, without explanations and rational interpretations."

As reported by Judith Ginzberg in *In search of a Voice: Working with Homeless Men*, music, ritual and dance can help the men to enhance self-esteem, establish trust, reduce tension, and promote group interaction

As a singer myself, I have often noticed how singing lifts my spirits. I also noticed that as I released and resolved anger, I discovered that I had a clearer, more resonant voice with greater range. My singing instructor claimed that a number of her students often experienced singer's "buzz" -a sense of joy and elation from singing. Apparently singing has been shown to increase levels of serotonin.

Keep in mind that you do not have to be a professional musician or singer to enjoy these benefits. The key is to accept whatever sounds you make without judgment. I often found that I could relax a great deal simply by playing whatever came to mind on my guitar. As the famous Beatles' song goes..."as my guitar gently weeps."

Expressing Yourself Verbally

To avoid resentment it is necessary for us to speak up about incidents as and when they occur. For some of us this may take some effort and practice. Not only must we speak up about irritants, we must also express our love and concern for others. When we let things slip by we end up internalizing them. They become harbored resentments that we will have to deal with at a later time.

To improve your emotional health, practice being less timid and set boundaries for yourself and others. You have a right to stand up for yourself and to speak up when anyone does something against you. It is usually easier to deal with an issue at the moment it happens, rather than later on , after you have stewed over it!

Writing and Journaling

Keep a Diary or Journal

Writing can be a great way to release emotional tension and promote healing. Putting thoughts down on paper can help clear the mind of its cobwebs. It is a great technique for getting our thoughts out of our head and onto paper where we can look at them more objectively. If you are afraid of someone reading it, then find a safe place for it or keep it under lock and key if that helps. Writing out our thoughts may seem strange to us at first, but with practice it will become easier and easier. Most of us wish they could faithfully keep a journal but realistically, few of us do. Simply be content to write in your journal whenever you feel like. It is unwise to create an expectation of writing faithfully. Be content with whatever and whenever you write.

Writing also has a second payoff as it allows us to look back over time and measure where we were a week, month or year ago. We will be able to note the progress we have made and the issues we have resolved. If an issue is still in our minds we can identify that we need to continue to work on it. Many times we resolve problems and forget about them. When we do so we tend to forget that we have made progress because we do not take note of the absence of the problem. Journaling helps us to look back and see from where we have come. Go out and purchase a journal for yourself. Pick one that has a cover that you like. Many stationery stores carry books with empty pages. Even if you do not plan to write today, purchase a journal so that it will be ready for you when you are ready.

Write or Tell Your Story

A larger writing project may involve writing a two or three page summary of your life story. This exercise can help in noticing the important events that have occurred in your life. In writing your story it is important to use "I" statements and to describe the feelings you had at each event. While therapeutic, this exercise has been known to be somewhat exhausting. Tackling it in portions can make the task a little easier. Many therapists ask their clients to write their story in order to get to know their client better.

Write Letters of Letting Go

There are times when we would like to express ourselves to someone yet conversations don't always go the way we want them to. We may also find that the other person will not listen or perhaps they are no longer around us to hear the communication. The person we wish to communicate with may be miles away, we may not even know their address, or for some of us they may have passed away.

Too often we have unfinished business with someone. Often we need closure. What we want to communicate may vary from relationship to relationship. We may be angry and hurt, or we may wish to tell someone that we love them and never told them. Writing a letter to that person can help us express our feelings and give closure.

More often than not we never end up sending the letter, but like keeping a diary or writing our story, writing a letter is an excellent way to get our thoughts and feelings out of our head. It helps greatly if we write the letter using the words "I feel..." in the letter rather than the finger pointing "You....".

Whether or not we ever send the letter is not important. What is important is the expression and release of our feelings. We can write the letter and then, with a clearer head, decide whether to send it or not. Keep in mind that the purpose of writing a letter is to provide release for ourselves, not to try to change someone else's thinking or behavior. What seems to be unfinished emotional business with someone else, is often an indication that we need to face something in ourselves.

Write the Letter You Would Like to Receive

Along with writing letters that we may never send we may wish to write the letter that we would like to receive. The letter we write should be the words of an apology we wish for or the words that we need to hear to obtain closure and to let go. After writing the letter we can read it back to ourselves and have a ceremony of completion.

Ceremonies of Completion and Letting Go

In some cases it may not be possible to send the letter we have written and often we may not want to. Keeping the letter in a drawer can often result in a lack of closure or a sense of holding on. To complete the unfinished business we can have our own ceremony of completion. By ripping the letter, shredding it or burning the letter in a fireplace, and saying a phrase to ourselves such as "I let go", we can have completion for ourselves.

The Empty Chair

It is often very healing to place an empty chair in front of us and imagine that the person you wish to communicate with is sitting in the chair. Proceeding to tell them exactly what we would like to say to them and how we are feeling is a technique often used in therapy. Our minds will be cleared through this opportunity to express ourselves. The next step is to imagine hearing them say what we would like to hear from them to help us heal.

Graveyard Visits - When Someone is no Longer With Us

Many of us have lost family members or friends. Again, we may have unfinished business. In some cases we may want to express our love, in other cases we may want to express our anger over their leaving us. Because someone has passed on does not mean that we should not be angry with him or her. Going to a graveyard and saying what we want to say can be a tremendously healing experience. Dr. Wayne Dyer described that going to his father's grave and expressing his anger and disappointments was a catalyst in creating his highly successful book *Your Erroneous Zones*. Go to a graveyard and say the things you want to say.

Physical and Emotional Catharsis

Massage and Healing Professions

In our emotional healing it is important to nurture ourselves and promote relaxation. Emotional expression involves the contraction and relaxation of muscle tissue and that emotional blocking leads to an increased level of muscular tension. Releasing the muscular tension will often help us release some of the emotional energy. A well-trained massage therapist will be able to assist in your healing process. Massage can bring about a better state of relaxation which in turn will bring about emotional release. Often one may find oneself moving through various emotions when receiving a massage. The latest research has indicated that touch and therefore massage, can result in an increase in serotonin.

Besides massage, there are a number of other healing professions such as acupuncture, reiki and aromatherapy. The choice of the service that you wish to receive is personal and what works for one may not be the choice of someone else. The key is to feel comfortable with what you are doing and to ensure that it promotes healing.

Crying and Crying Substitutes

Often tears well up but we do not give ourselves permission to cry. We may experience tension in the chest and throat area, but we do not cry. Often it is very easy to stifle the tears and continue on with our tasks rather than express our feelings. If we pay attention to these signals and give ourselves permission to cry and let go, then crying will usually follow. Noticing our breath at these times can also help us let the tears flow.

In many cases though, we may not be ready for tears and may develop our own crying substitutes. Often, adults will learn whole repertoires to substitute for crying Simply talking and sharing in a support group may be one of the first stages in allowing release to occur. If the individual's tension level lowers, and he or she experiences enough self acceptance, then tears will likely follow.

Sobbing or Crying

The earliest tears will be usually experienced with tension in the upper chest and throat however a deeper type of release is possible. Crying can often lead to a deeper sobbing if we accept the pain we are feeling and allow the tears to fully flow. This type of release is centered more in the stomach area and will involve more of the body, particularly the abdomen and shoulders. A deep body sob promotes healing and is a deeper release of emotional tension. The sobbing with the whole body can be quite exhausting and a period of rest afterward is a good idea.

I clearly remember a time when some painful memories were triggered while watching a movie with a friend. I became aware of a deep rooted sense of loneliness and pain that had long been forgotten. I asked my friend to stop the tape and she held me as I cried. As I took deep breaths, the crying came from deep within my chest. I could feel a knot of energy being released from deep inside of me. Although painful and exhausting, I had acknowledged a deep sense of pain which my friend reflected back to me when she said "you've really been hurt". After resting, I felt a sense of calmness and serenity, and of course, a stronger connection with my friend for supporting me through this.

Laughter

While tears are often credited with healing, so is laughter. Rent a funny movie, go to see a comedian, or call a friend with whom you share laughter. Finding humor in our own situation or mannerisms helps us to accept ourselves. Laughter can restore vitality and produce chemical changes in our bodies. Laughter reduces our susceptibility to disease and enhances our coping abilities.

Make Use of Emotional Movies etc.

Often we can bring about healing tears by making use of emotional movies or music. If you find that some sentimental movie, a piece of music, or a poem helps you to cry then, by all means, use it. Sometimes all we need is a little extra to help get the release started. Sometimes a movie or song will trigger a memory or release for reasons that may be unknown to us. Seize the moment as an opportunity to let go and be free of whatever has been bottled up. Keep a box of tissue handy and let go! Remember too, that we can also use various forms of entertainment to help us laugh.

Creative Visualization

Visualizing a Different Outcome

Creative visualization is a powerful technique that can help us move into the type of lifestyle we wish to have. It can also help us develop a more positive attitude or assist us in the development of a sense of competence and serenity in dealing with others. There is some sound wisdom in the words "whatever you tell yourself and believe is then true for you." Using techniques of visualization, we can work on our beliefs and begin to train our mind to operate with new beliefs about ourselves. By visualizing ourselves being successful, so we become. If we imagine ourselves being relaxed around others, it is likely that we will become that way. There are numerous books on creative visualization, meditation, and affirmations. You may even want to create your own affirmations!

The Birth Order Exercise

A wonderful technique for promoting understanding of family issues and discovering the humanness of our parents and family members is to guide ourselves through the following exercise.

Imagine your parents as they were when they met. Imagine the conditions they were living under when they married. Go on and imagine what it would have been like if you had been born in the order you wish you had been born in. With each birth, imagine the circumstances and stresses on the family. Then imagine the way it actually happened. What were your parent's emotional states? What would the state of each of the other family members be? The purpose of the exercise is not to release others from responsibility for their actions but to gain a better understanding of where we came and the climate in which we were raised.

Cultural and Religious Healing Practices

With the exception of the Native Indians, North Americans are one of the few cultures who lack a healing ceremony. Native Indians practice and participate in various healing rituals such as sweat lodges, and talking circles. Other cultures have various beliefs and practices that promote healing. Various religions have services that are related to healing. Learn more about what your culture or religion may have to offer you. Again, our healing is personal, therefore what one chooses may be different from another. Discover what works for you.

Healing Principles

The following are principles that will help greatly in our emotional recovery. I would suggest that you make a list of the headings and place the list somewhere to remind yourself of them on a regular basis. These are principles and tools that have allowed me to progress through the process of emotional recovery.

Facing the Truth

One of the prime rules of healing is that healing cannot occur if we are mired in denial of the truth of the hurtful event. Denial serves a purpose in protecting us from the pain when we are not ready to deal with it, but often we end up using denial without being aware of its consequences. Denial often prevents us from healing.

In examining any event we must be willing to accept the truth about it. For example, we may have to accept that we were laid off, that we felt rejected, lonely or isolated, or let down by ourselves or others. We may simply have to acknowledge that indeed we were hurt.

Healing is a process of telling ourselves the truth. We may have felt pain, shame, fear, loss, or helplessness, or we may have felt anger. We need to face these truths and realities of the situation in order to allow healing to take place. Often we may have to own up to secrets that we have hidden from ourselves and others. Often it is our secrets that cause us the most pain. We do not need to reveal them to others but we need to be truthful to ourselves. A big part of healing is self-forgiveness.

Modifying Defeatist Behaviors

In our emotional healing process we often become aware of various self-defeating behaviors or habits that limit our ability to develop a sense of self-esteem. The development of self-esteem is a crucial component in identifying many of the contradictions and falsehoods that we have erroneously believed about harmful events. Identifying the true nature of the perpetrators and increasing our self worth brings about release and healing. Self-esteem is a sense of self that develops in small portions, like building blocks, on top of each other. Building a stronger foundation of self-esteem allows us to see the contradictions of our hurtful events.

Too often we sabotage or undermine our own self-esteem with behaviors that stem from our attempts to get deserved love and attention. Too often we do one or more of the following:

- addictively seek approval
- allow others to determine our worth
- addictively and dependently seek love
- set unreasonable goals and expectations of ourselves and others
- avoid setting boundaries
- we give away personal power
- minimize the positives
- exaggerate our experiences to make them seem more impressive
- engage in black and white or all or nothing thinking
- generalize our experience using words such as always, everybody or nobody, instead of sometimes or some people.
- using the word "should" too often (referred to as "shoulding on yourself")
- expect perfection from ourselves and others

All of the above behaviors can diminish our sense of self-esteem and can prevent us from developing a spiritual and emotional backbone. Developing a backbone is done by keeping our personal power and setting boundaries with others so that we can choose when we wish to let someone be involved with ourselves. The key to a backbone is the ability to make choices and follow through with them.

Often when we are confronting our own issues we end up confronting behavior in others; moreover, we need to decide what our own standards of acceptable behavior are. We can then use this yardstick to measure how we are being treated in relationships. Confronting the inappropriate behavior of others can be a challenging prospect and often requires that we go out of our comfort zone. When challenged to do so, we often feel intimidated and fearful. It is difficult to focus on the whole situation. When we face a difficult situation with a person we find difficult, we can increase our chances of success by feeling our own breath and our own feet on the floor, and by seeing the person and focusing on the space around him or her as well. If we do this we can maintain our sense of strength and accomplish the boundary-setting we wish to achieve.

In order to achieve emotional healing, it is necessary to bring an end to the behaviors that are contributing to our own sadness. Constantly going over an event without re-examining the context will only serve to re-stimulate hurt and sadness. Similarly, negative thinking can be a habit that is contributing to our sadness. If this is the case, then we need to counter our negative thoughts with positive ones.

Taking the time at the end of the day to note three positive things that happened, no matter how small, will help us to learn how to notice the positives. We may have trouble noticing the positives simply because we have been overly proficient at noticing the negatives without developing the skill of noticing and giving weight to the positives. If we do not come up with any positives, then this is an indication of how undeveloped our skill is in this area.

If we practice noticing the positives, then in time we will become more positive. It will also train us to value the positive things in our lives. If we fight the idea of stating positives, then perhaps this is an indication of anger that needs to be resolved. Noticing the positives does not mean denying the hurt or the negatives in our lives; it simply means giving weight to both and attempting to achieve a better balance of recognition of the negative and positive things going on in our day-to-day lives.

Believing in a Purpose for All Things that Happen

In healing, an important concept to consider is a willingness to believe in a higher power. This higher power can be whatever we want it to be. A higher power is something we define ourselves. Some of us may have discarded our earlier images of a God, while some of us may not even believe in a God. What we need to believe in, however, is that there is some force in this universe that is greater than we are and that it will protect us, help us with our issues and bring us what we need to go through the process of healing.

As we begin to unlock our pain we learn that we can trust that our environment will provide us with the people, events, materials, and awareness that we need to heal. Some call this synchronicity or serendipity, while others call it coincidence. The common factor is that if we are committed to healing then our environment will bring us what we need as we are ready.

While some of us may be reluctant to accept the notion of a higher power or God, the key word here is to be willing. Willingness will let us be open to the possibility that the right things will happen at the right time to help us along our path to emotional health. According to Steven Covey, author of *The Seven Habits of Highly Successful People*, most successful people believe that events happen for a purpose. When we are in the healing process, events in our lives will likely help us to better understand ourselves better and to resolve our issues. The right relationship will come along, losses may occur, or changes in our life will happen. They will especially occur if we are willing to believe that there is a greater purpose or a higher power helping us in our quest for emotional and spiritual health.

During the times when I was at my lowest, there was always some special little event or person that appeared to help when I needed help. One afternoon I was feeling quite low, yet decided to go out and buy some posters to brighten up my apartment. As I was driving back from the store I pulled up to a red light at an intersection. While waiting for the light to change, a family crossed the street. A little boy looked at me and saw that I was not very happy. He waved to me and mouthed the words "It's going to be OK!" The parents noticed that he was speaking to a stranger and whisked him along, but my higher power had done its work through this child. The boy's message carried me for weeks and I still feel encouraged when I think of this event!

I know that in the last few years I have always received what I needed to continue the process of healing. I did not always get exactly what I asked for, but I did get what I needed. I remember being very frustrated with my employer. While confiding to my friend Diane about my troubles, she jokingly said "Mark, the solution to your problems is to get laid. I'm going to say a prayer to this Higher Power that you get laid." The next day I called Diane back with the news that I had gotten laid off. I joked that she should be a little more specific with her prayers next time. A common saying in 12-step groups is "be careful what you ask for, you might just get it, but it may not be exactly what you had in mind!" Although the loss of employment was not an enjoyable experience, it was the push I needed to change careers. In a way, it was exactly what I needed and it happened at the appropriate time.

In our healing process, we can trust that things will happen to us when we are ready. Although we may feel tested and strained at times, we are given only what we can handle, as was always my case. This has been said many times by people working on recovery in various 12-step groups. We will be protected from feelings and knowledge that we are not yet ready to deal with. Our mind plays a very important role in subconsciously deciding what we are ready to deal with and letting us know when we are ready. If something happens or if we gain knowledge about something, it is usually because we are ready.

I firmly believe that if we are committed to working on our issues, then our environment will collaborate with us. It will bring about the appropriate circumstances required to face these issues and develop the insight we need to resolve them and move on to our next issue.

Developing and Maintaining a Sense of Hope

Whenever we undertake a project or task it is usually done with a sense of hope that there will be rewards for our efforts. In an emotional recovery there will be times when we are making progress. At other times we may seem stuck and feel that we are making little progress, if any at all. In revealing our pain to ourselves and releasing it, it is easy to lose sight of the fact that things will get better. In times of trouble we must remind ourselves of the progress we have made.

Mark Linden O'Meara

Often, we may feel overwhelmed by our problems and at times some people may even feel suicidal. If these thoughts occur, then it is helpful to try to alleviate the feelings of being overwhelmed. This can be accomplished by trying to identify the issues that are causing the greatest amount of stress in our life, discovering alternative ways of dealing with distress, reducing the amount of self criticism and "shoulds" we generate, and breaking problems down into their smaller components. We need to remind ourselves that these problems shall eventually pass.

We must make an effort to notice that although we may have a lot of work to do and things may seem bleak, there is a light at the end of tunnel. We can recover from our past injuries and begin to feel joy again. When times get tough we can reach out to a friend, or if necessary call the local distress center. There is always hope, even if we must look for it. Others have gone through difficult processes such as ours and are willing to help. Recovery is possible when we maintain a sense of hope!

Respecting Others

In our effort to recover emotionally we may uncover anger that will need to be dealt with. Sometimes it will be necessary to express our feelings by writing a letter or telling how we are feeling to someone. In our recovery it is very important to respect others' feelings and wishes as well as our own.

Others may not be ready to hear what we have to say about themselves therefore we must make certain that we keep the focus on ourselves. It may be necessary to confront someone if he or she has harmed or hurt us, but if they tell us that they do not want us to communicate with them then we must respect their wishes.

The old adage "two wrongs do not make a right" is critical in achieving emotional health. Attacking someone verbally or writing a scathing letter only serves to vent emotion not resolve it. It reduces our personal power and worth. If we are to communicate our feelings to someone who has hurt us we must do it with compassion and respect the other person's wishes. I do not mean that we must be under that person's control, but if the other person indicates that he or she does not want us to contact them, we must respect this. This is particularly true in dating relationships. Often we must respect boundaries that other people set. If someone does not wish to communicate with us then there are other ways to resolve our emotions which have been described in this book.

Establishing a Connection with Nature

In the last one hundred years mankind has lost most of its opportunity to experience nature as previous generations have. Few city people have seen the millions of stars that light up the sky on a clear night, away from the light pollution of the city. Fewer have experienced the quiet, non-judgmental, peaceful sound of nature. Try to find a place that you can go to - a park or arboretum. Try taking a day trip now and then. If getting to nature is not possible, then perhaps you can bring nature to yourself. Get some plants or put up posters, or purchase a meditative sound recording that will remind you of the beauty of nature and its healing properties. Nature does not judge our pain, sorrow, anger, or joy.

Developing a Support System

A key element of emotional recovery is developing your own support system. Although you may not have discovered this before, there are many kind people who are willing to help you and be a friend to you. To find these people we need to communicate our needs. If we are hurting we may need to take a perceived risk and let someone know that we are hurting. Even if we are very perceptive of other people's emotional state we must accept that others are not mind readers. If we are hurting and need comfort, we need to communicate these needs to others. Be honest. If we want someone to go out for a coffee with us or to spend some time with us, ask him or her; but also give the person the freedom to say no.

If you are lonely, find a support group you can join. In a support group we can share ideas, hopes and thoughts with others who are working on similar issues, and we can also listen and learn from others. Most groups usually have a list of people to call should the need arise. If you are not sure of whether you like the group, go for a few times (six meetings are suggested). If you do not like it, you can always stop, but if you do not go at all, you will miss finding out what a group can do for you. For many of us, joining a group is a big step, therefore it is important to find a group that we are comfortable with. If the group seems inappropriate, then try another one until you find the group that you are comfortable with. The important thing is to at least try a group for a while and then, with first-hand knowledge and experience of the group, you can decide if you wish to continue or not.

Try also to find one or two friends with whom you can talk to openly and honestly with. This may take some time to develop, but if you have a friend who will listen and help guide you, your healing process will be greatly enhanced. Most support groups provide telephone lists of people willing to discuss issues with members. The sharing among members helps them to learn from each other and provides comfort in understanding that they are not alone in their problems.

Keep in mind that although our healing process is a very personal thing, sharing our feelings during this time can lead to greater trust and better relationships later on! Sharing and allowing others to help us will enhance the recovery of yourself and others. In an article titled *The Broken Heart*, James Lynch describes how communication plays a vitally important role in our health. He writes "The rhythm of a heart beat of a patient in a coronary care unit can be altered when the patient is touched by another human being. This occurs in patients in deep coma as well as in those who are fully conscious." Communication allows us to share thoughts, ideas, hopes, and feelings.

Personal Attitudes and the Healing Process

Notice the Little Things

Very few of us frequently have events in our lives that rate extremely high on an emotional scale. A marriage, a birth, winning a lottery or a contest are wonderful events but they do not occur with great frequency (at least not for the author!). Troublesome events such as losses, illnesses, etc., seem to occur more frequently and are usually considered to be traumatic in nature. How do we achieve some balance? We can achieve balance by looking for and noticing the smaller nice things that happen to us. Sometimes this takes practice and we may need to get into the habit of doing this. At the end of each day, make a mental note of three nice things that happened to you during the day, however trivial they may seem. I guarantee this habit will start to lift you up!

Give up Control

Many of us believe that we are in control of our emotions. When we have stuffed or suppressed our emotions, it is really our emotions that are in control of us! Many of us are afraid that if we begin to let go, we may lose control. Since we have become so good at turning off our emotions we are usually able to do so when the need arises. As we begin to experience our emotional selves again, we still have the ability to numb out if feelings get too strong for us to deal with.

Allow Yourself to Get Angry

Anger tends to be the emotion we fear the most, however, anger is really just an indication to ourselves that we are being hurt, or violated in some way according to our standards and principles. For this reason anger is considered a secondary emotion. It is a response to our hurt. When we are angry we usually need to look at the underlying cause and the hurting that is going on within us. Eventually, our anger can be resolved by expressing it and getting in touch with the pain and crying it out.

Let Go of the Fear

In the beginning of this process we may fear that if we begin to let go and release our emotions, we will not be able to stop. Remember that for a long time we have been able to hold our emotions at bay. We can still use that skill if need be. Try getting in touch with a small bit of sadness and see if you can immediately shut if off again. It is likely that you are able to do this. Most of us do have control of our emotions. We have the ability to turn them off at will. Turning them on has been our problem.

Do Things in Moderation

It is important to do things in moderation. If we have been keeping ourselves extremely busy, then slow down gradually. If we are driving a car 60 miles an hour and all of a sudden slam on the brakes, it creates havoc for the traffic behind us. The same is true if we need to slow ourselves down. Coming to an abrupt halt may be overwhelming. Start limiting your activities or begin turning down new requests. Use the free time to try to relax. The paradox of the busy person is that he or she is hurting and needs to slow down but slowing down can result in beginning to hurt more. Moderation is the answer.

It may also be a time when we will want to put off major decisions until our emotional state has stabilized. We may have a great deal of energy available to us when we release unresolved emotions, however given that we are in a process of recovery, major decisions may only add to our stress. A move or change of employment, unless forced upon us, may create unnecessary upheaval when we need to find some anchors in our lives at this time. A technique to improve our sense of grounding is to sit in a chair with our feet on the floor, breathing deeply, and focusing on the sensation of our feet firmly planted on the ground below us.

Be Patient

How does one eat an elephant? ...One bite at a time! Our recovery is the same. Many small steps or bites add up to recovery. Accept that full recovery takes time. Healing may take months or even years. It is not something we can accomplish with a quick fix or a weekend seminar, although in one week we can make great progress. Be patient and give yourself time. Notice the little steps you have made and how they have added up!

Accept How Things Turn Out

Sometimes things turn out differently from what we had hoped for. Often we get what we need rather than what we ask for, and often we lack the wisdom to see this. Accepting what we get can be a very important recovery tool, especially if we believe that there is a master plan for our recovery that is being managed by a power that is greater than ourselves.

Sometimes we do not get the job or relationship that we want or we get something else. In the long run many people say that the pain they went through or the way things worked out was exactly what they needed in their lives at a certain time to overcome a hurdle or to learn something special about themselves.

Let Your Recovery be Personal

Each of our own paths in recovery is unique and belongs to only us. There are many things we share but each of our circumstances is unique in some way. Our process is the same. What works for one may not be what we choose. What works for us may not be how someone else may approach recovery. Some of us are artists while some are writers. Some may use massage while some may use other alternative methods. We learn to share with others and to listen, but we develop our own set of tools for recovery. We are unique and we can develop a sense of what works for us.

Accept Yourself As An Emotional Being

One of the characteristics that makes us human is our ability to feel emotions. If you have been taught to hide your emotions you likely have some negative self talk going on in your mind when you begin to feel emotional. Try to change your self talk. Do not put yourself down for being emotional. Accept it as part of being human. Notice how movies, music and most forms of entertainment affect our emotions. Instead of shunning your emotional side, embrace it and welcome it into your life again. Your emotions can be your friend!

Accept that Emotions are Not Logical

If we were truly logical beings, then we would not likely have our emotions play such a large part in our lives. The fact is that emotions are not logical. We can be angry at someone, and love him or her at the same time. Our emotions deny logic. Accepting this allows us to feel the emotions without judging ourselves as being crazy.

In times of release we may be surprised by how much

emotion is available to be released. We may find our patterns of behavior and consciousness shifting as we let go of what we have held onto for so long. Accept that the process will take place and that we can survive without control and logic.

Trust Your Intuition

Sometimes we may have a feeling that we should call someone, be at a certain place, or make a particular choice for no logical reason other than a gut feeling. Usually, these intuitive feelings turn out to be correct if we can measure the outcome. Sometimes we cannot measure the outcome so we may not know what the consequences of our actions were. In our recovery it is important to follow our intuition.

One Saturday evening I was watching a movie with a friend and I had a very strong intuitive feeling to go to a dance that a friend of mine operated. I had been experiencing this feeling all day long. I explained to my friend that I had to go somewhere. I went to the dance and met someone who, a week later, gave me a book that was crucial to my recovery. If I had not followed my intuition, my recovery would have taken a lot longer and I probably would not have received what I needed at the time I needed it. Learn to trust those gut feelings.

Take the Time That it Takes

Some things take longer than others to get over. It is important to give yourself as much time as you need to get over a loss or an event that triggers emotion. It is not how long you go out with someone that determines the amount of time it takes to get over a loss but how much that person affected you and how much you cared for him or her. Some people have a great impact on us in a short period. Healing will take as long as it takes. A study by psychiatrist Glen Davidson suggests that the length of time to grieve varies greatly, from 18 to 24 months. It can even be longer for some losses and some situations, without being considered abnormal.

Seeing the Positive in Losses

Although often difficult to imagine, positive things can come from losses. Often we learn a lesson or are assisted in releasing and resolving deeper issues. A few years ago I had a cat named Shadow. I got Shadow as a kitten in my second year of university. She had always seemed to sense when I was having a difficult time emotionally and would sort of wimper and curl up beside me. I remember when my father died. Shadow came into my room and placed her paws on my knees as I sat on the edge of the bed, and strained up with a sad but comforting tone in her meow. One morning I got up to go to work and Shadow did not answer my calls. I found her lying on the living room floor, her lifeless body missing the energy that had made her so special. It was a great loss.

I kept wondering why this had to happen. I had just started into working through my issues and this just didn't seem fair. I had a few good cries, got angry, even denied my loss in my dreams, but then finally I accepted my loss. I then realized that for the first time in my life, I had gone through a grieving process and had actually healed from the loss - an extremely important lesson to learn.

A few years later I volunteered with a seniors resource center. I was matched up with a kind gentleman named Victor who had recently lost his wife. We conversed many times and while he had opinions of his own, he was also respectful of other peoples opinions. A few months later my friend Victor passed away. He had greatly missed his wife. His obituary contained this quote from Sir Henry Woolton: "she first deceased; he for a little tried, to live without her, liked it not, and died." The description of Victor's own loss moved me and I was also deeply affected by his death. The loss triggered my own unresolved grief. I was aware that in grieving my loss of his companionship, I was also grieving my own losses - that of a high school friend, and of the deaths of my parents. Denying my grief would have locked in my pain. Again, events happened for a reason.

Work on the Problem not on the Symptoms

For a long time I tried as hard as I could to feel happy. I tried positive thinking, seminars, etc. I also worked on communication, my loneliness and isolation, negative attitudes, as well as numerous other problems that arose from being emotionally numb. The resolution to most of these problems came from working on the main problem that I was experiencing, namely the suppression of all my emotions from a very early age. Keep your focus on the main problem at hand. As you make progress in your emotional recovery you will likely find that the symptoms will become less and less noticeable!

Remember that You are a Survivor

Often we need to remind ourselves that we have the strength and courage to face our problems and pain. We are much bigger and greater than our problems, although at times we may feel overwhelmed. Our pains may be great and at times frightening, but we can overcome them. Remember that, as with all feelings that are allowed to follow their course, they shall pass. We can and will heal if we have courage and if we trust the healing process. This often requires courage, but if during our dark times we remind ourselves of our progress, then we can encourage ourselves to continue our healing process.

Go at an Appropriate Pace

The purpose in therapy is to hold a mirror up to ourselves. Often a therapist or a friend will try to guide us in opening up our blind spots. It is important that we set boundaries and agreements as to how far we can be pushed to discover things about ourselves.

Identifying too many issues at once can cause an ignition of emotions that may be overwhelming and hard on our health. Our issues can be like a pack of matches - we take one match at a time and light it. If we were to light all the matches at once, the package will erupt in flames in an uncontrolled and dangerous flash of intensity. Our own issues can be similar. We need to look at a few issues at a time and deal with them without being overwhelmed and overloaded. Go at an appropriate pace. Our minds and our environment will help us bring issues as we are ready.

Set Goals

Both children and adults need to feel a sense of purpose in our day-to-day living. We need a sense of achievement or a sense that we are moving toward some ideal. Setting goals helps us to attain a sense of purpose. For many people in the healing process, their goal is to resolve some of their issues. This in itself can be a very noble goal and a source of inspiration. In setting goals, it is important to ensure that the goals are realistic, measurable and attainable. If you do not have any goals, try choosing a few small goals and identify the steps you can take to achieve them.

Have Fun

A journey of healing can be a great time of learning. Many support groups are filled with the sound of joyous laughter, even with the serious nature of the issues that the participants are working on. Healing periods can be a time of learning and a time of joy and fun. Develop your sense of playfulness and allow yourself to be silly at times. When discussing his acting skills, Tom Hanks said that the best actors are those who allow the child in themselves to have a big role in their acting. Sometimes we have to remind ourselves and allow ourselves to feel more joy. Let your spirit to soar!

If you love something,
Set it free.
If it comes back,
It's probably co-dependent!

Mark Linden O'Meara

Dealing with Loneliness

The Roots of Loneliness

It has been said time and time again that we are born alone and we die alone. Although at times we may feel alone, there is a difference between being alone and being lonely. Although we may live in a city with thousands of people, loneliness is a very common problem. I once spoke with the director of a crisis line who advised me that over 60 percent of calls to their lines were due to social isolation and loneliness. The issue of loneliness is rampant throughout our society. Loneliness can be the root of many personal problems. Retired psychologist Boris Blai Jr. states that "investigations ...show a connection between loneliness and depression, substance abuse, suicide and other forms of psycho-pathology." Blai also describes two types of loneliness: a feeling of aching due to the absence of an attachment figure; the other a sense of being excluded or not being accepted in some form of community. Blai states "there is also some evidence that either form of loneliness is more apt to be present when the lonely individual suffers from feelings of low self-assurance." Research has indicated that it is one's attitudes and sense of self-esteem that have a greater impact on ones sense of belonging rather than the number of clubs one joins.

For myself, loneliness has been a major issue as well. For the last 10 years I have experienced little or no family support. My mother died when I was 23 and my father died five years later. Due to our upbringing, my brothers have not remained close. As a result of my lack of family, I was always feeling a sense of emptiness and disconnection. Although I have become involved in a number of volunteer organizations and made a number of friends, I was still experiencing a strong sense of loneliness and aching regarding the loss of a parental figure, as Blai described. I have since learned that my attitudes and beliefs play a greater role in dealing with loneliness than I had previously thought possible. I have discovered that a strong and healthy relationship with myself is critical. I had to examine whether I could be comfortable with myself when alone, and whether I could become my own parent. I also had to review the nature of people and learn to accept the nature of society and then adjust my attitudes appropriately.

Whether we have living parents or not, many of us have experienced a separation from our families of origin. In the case of abusive parents, part of the solution to our problems has been to strike out on our own and to forge healthier relationships. In some cases, it is healthier to be away from our families of origin than to participate in the dysfunction and denial of issues. Perhaps at times our need to remove ourselves from the family situation will only be temporary. In either case, a question remains regarding how we can obtain support and friendship and find a community in which we can also give.

Although some of us have been able to find a sense of familiarity with friends or perhaps a mentor, it can be difficult to maintain long-term support. Friendships can be very fluid. Just as I change and grow, so do friends. I have learned to recognize that friends may move, change interests, pursue other friendships, or may be unavailable perhaps due to the demands of their work or study.

There is also the need to recognize that any one friend cannot meet all of my needs and that at any one time I may need a number of different friendships. In addition, some friends may be acquaintances, others may be more close, while others may be friends that I can share my deepest thoughts and feelings with. One may be a partner or lover. I have often heard that most people have only two or three close friends and that these friendships take time to develop. This may prove advantageous, since a smaller number of close friends is more likely to provide a greater sense of belonging than a larger number of acquaintances.

Developing friendships also involves developing the ability to choose our friends appropriately. If we are not selective in our choice of friends, then we can often be disappointed. Too often, perhaps due to previous patterns of loneliness, we end up being friends with whomever will reciprocate our friendliness. Once we realize that there really is an abundant number of possible friendships out there for us, we can learn to be more choosy. I have also learned that diversification in friends can be beneficial. Where previously, as the saying goes, we may have put all our eggs in one basket. The same holds true for the places that we meet our friends. It can be helpful to develop a number of interests and goals that bring us into contact with a variety of people. If we choose to give up a particular activity, we do not end up losing our base of friendships.

With regard to creating friendships, I have learned that being open is a first step. I've also learned that it takes time to develop a sense of trust and openness. At one time I was like a closed book with very little self-disclosure. Then came a period when I was open with whomever would listen. I have since learned that sharing intense feelings can scare some people away. I then began to develop the skill of testing the waters with friendships. I have learned that there is a difference between being open and seeking help for my problems. When starting friendships, a certain amount of openness will draw others to me. However, seizing new friendships as an opportunity for unloading problems can scared people away. At some times, it is necessary to put on a mask with others.

While we need support, it is important to look in the appropriate places. Although we are often asked how we are doing, answering honestly can frighten others away. The outpouring of our problems can result in receiving less support than if we had been able to simply spend time with someone without actually discussing our problems. During the final editing phase of this book, I experienced a number of financial setbacks and the loss of a wonderful pet. During this time a fellow student and I would go for coffee. The sense of encouragement and support I felt from this person occurred without directly bringing up the losses. I believe this situation is an example of a popular 12-step group saying. AA members and Al-anon members are often hear the phrase "fake it till you make it". I now believe that sometimes it is appropriate to withhold issues from others. Just as if we are over-watering a plant, a substantial outpouring can drown the seed of friendship. How then, can we be truthful to ourselves and others when we are asked how we are doing? Perhaps another 12-step saying is appropriate. If someone asks you how are you doing, we can answer "fine", while remembering that "fine" stands for "F*cked up, Insecure, Neurotic and Emotional!

It is important to remember that, as human beings, we often have limits as to the degree of support we can give. If we are constantly in need of support and constantly focusing on our problems, then others may shy away from us since their own limits are being reached. We may also be triggering their issues. Friendships are complex. Rarely do two people say "I have a problem, can we be friends?", but over the sharing of interests and values, we come to know and trust one another. We learn to give and receive from our friends in a manner that is appropriate for the level of friendship. We also learn to let go.

Unconscious Bargains

The creation of this chapter came about after a challenging time when a number of friendships ended in disintegration. It was a very painful time, as I learned how I had essentially built some of these friendships out of neediness rather than on the basis of who these people were and why I had chosen them as friends. I have learned that neediness can cause the loss of our discriminating guide in who we choose as friends. Because of my need for someone to tell me that I was OK, essentially I was making an unconscious bargain with these people that I would do something for them and in return, they would be my friend. It is no wonder then, with the lesson I needed to learn, that these friendships vanished. In examining my remaining friendships, I realized that these were based on an equality of needs as well as a greater willingness to support each other. This process of discovery led me to face a problem that had been following me around for a number of years. As my friend Bruce put it, "this is your beast or shadow that you need to tame or learn to live with".

As a result, I was in a sense trying to find a sense of family in friendships, acquaintances and people I met. It was the searching in others for this sense of belonging and love that reflected an un-resolvable neediness. This was my beast or shadow. I also learned that I was ashamed of my current loneliness as well as being ashamed of the loneliness I experienced as a child and teenager. These dynamics seemed to create too heavy a burden and ongoing sense of sadness, loss and depression.

After the loss of three friendships, and recognizing that it was necessary to resolve this problem, I sought to identify ways of nurturing myself and to become my own best friend. I realized that I needed to develop my own self-parenting and nurturing skills and to accept that I was in fact alone and at times, always will be. Ironically, doing so has created the sense of wholeness that had eluded me for so long!

While I do not expect to always be alone, I am learning that I can be comfortable with myself and self-loving. I am learning to lean on myself more, rather than to seek my sense of worth and validation from others. In doing so, I feel more complete and stronger, and better equipped to enter a relationship or friendship. Instead of developing friendships in the hope of cementing over or filling in the emptiness, I am recognizing the needs I have and the things I have to offer and how I may be able to contribute equally in a friendship. Sometimes the best way to develop a friendship is to be a friend to someone rather than looking for a friend for yourself.

It is also important to note the role that synchronicity and timing play in meeting new friends. Sometimes we are just at the right time and in the right frame of mind. Having learned a number of valuable lessons, I took some time off to integrate and went to a small island for a retreat. While there I happened to meet a friend I hadn't seen in a while and also met up with another traveler. Many people have echoed the thought that we often meet special people at the time we are ready. After this challenging time, my Graduate Advisor jokingly said, "finally, fate is working for you." Looking back, I believe it always was.

Neediness

I have often found that it is most easy to attract friends into my life when I am in a positive frame of mind. With the exception of people I have met in support groups, this support is hardest to find when I am down and in need of nurturing. It has been interesting to note the habits of other people in times of trouble. I have observed that quite often people will withdraw and retreat rather than lean on others for support. This is an important concept to keep in mind when looking for support from others who are going through difficult times. Although the support of others can be beneficial, there are times when we and others need to retreat for a period of self-discovery. This self-discovery period may be a time of re-discovering one's goals, reconnecting or examining one's purpose. Having experienced this period of loneliness, we often emerge stronger and more aware of our desires and capabilities. We often develop a stronger sense of self and personal strength. Often the reality of loneliness is less painful than the fear of being alone.

The paradox of loneliness lies in the notion that the more accepting we are of our aloneness, the more likely we will be able to attract people into our lives. Unfortunately, it seems that neediness is not a valued commodity in relationships. People seem to have an uncanny ability to sense neediness in others. While it is important to be able to express our needs to others, this is not, however, to be confused with neediness. Neediness is an inability to nurture ourselves, to be incomplete on our own, a strong requirement to have someone else fill an emptiness inside ourselves or an attempt at avoiding responsibility for parenting ourselves. As my friend Daniel told me, "there is a subtle difference between wanting to be helped and wanting to help yourself". People tend to want to help those who are in the process of working on solutions to their problems. In developmental terms, we may not have matured to the point where we have developed our own autonomy and self-direction. Like the child who says "hey, look at what I did", we may lack the ability to give ourselves the acknowledgment we need.

The Developed Self

I think we have all heard some variation of the phrase "you have to solve your own problems before you get into a relationship". Although it is impossible to solve all of your problems before getting into a relationship, it is important to have a healthy sense of one's values and the gifts you have to offer others. This is the essence of self-esteem. I believe it is also healthy to have developed a sense of one's interests and talents, which will then assist in the creation of suitable friendships outside of the relationship. I have often heard from people that when a relationship ends, they find themselves very alone, having given up many of their friends and interests. In love, we sometimes devote ourselves totally to the other person.

Perhaps the following can illustrate a healthier attitude towards the maintenance of the individuals in relationships. At some weddings a ritual is followed involving the lighting of a larger candle from two candles, and the extinguishing of both of the smaller candles. The romantic thought is that the two people are now joined as one and that the individual lights are merged. Yet in reality there are really still two people who have different interests, needs, goals, and communication skills. I have recently witnessed ceremonies in which the new couple leaves the two individual candles burning with the larger candle representing the light of the relationship between them. Whether married or simply dating, the lesson that often needs to be learned is that it is unhealthy to totally lose one's sense of self in a relationship. Too often, one of the partners begins to grow, touching off a reaction of issues and changes.

With regard to having to solve your problems before getting into a relationship, I believe a more appropriate statement is that one's chances of a successful relationship will increase if he or she recognizes that one has an emptiness and can learn to fill that hole before getting into the relationship. Human beings are a social race. We need community, connectedness and support. These three aspects of our social lives are experienced differently when we seek them to fulfill an emptiness rather than to love and give to others. Resolving past issues and losses also helps. When we walk into a relationship or friendship with a cleaner slate built upon a more solid foundation of self, relationships work out better and healthier.

In examining my own situation, I made an important discovery regarding my expression of emotion that has impacted the nuance of my friendships and relationships. It is important to recognize that we may be doing our own healing work at the times we are meeting new friends and becoming involved in organizations. I came to realize that much of my emotional energy was being directed at these people with the expectation that they would help me deal with it, resolve it or simply acknowledge it. In this essence I was needing to have my emotions validated by others and was therefore once again needy. Since a substantial part of communication is non-verbal, I have learned that it is important to learn to own the emotional energy and be able to appropriately direct it through other forms of release. This is a subtle concept. When we are aware of our own emotional energy we can learn how to direct it and release it appropriately. This can allow others to feel less burdened in their endeavor to support our healing work.

Replacing Lost Family

As discussed earlier, for a number of years I have had to cope with not having a sense of family. This is also recognized as a common occurrence in many adult children and victims of sexual abuse, where family ties may have been severed. Since family is considered to be an important aspect of being human, how does one replace the nurturing and comfort that we can give and receive in families? In the following paragraphs I discuss a number of concepts regarding this issue. Although these suggestions have helped me, I believe there is no single or perfect answer to the problem. Take what you feel will help from this chapter!

Although loneliness can often bring about a sense of failure, it is important to recognize the nature of society. First of all, it can be difficult to find support, particularly when we are needy. People often don't know how to respond empathically when we express our feelings. Quite often I've been told by well meaning people that I shouldn't feel so bad because others don't have family, or that others don't see their family. Although people's intentions are good, I have learned to recognize that these statements, as true as they are, do nothing to recognize my own sense of loss. On the other hand, the message that "without family, life is empty" reverberates in church halls, on TV shows and is communicated to us time and time again during holiday seasons. How then does one cope with not having a real sense of family?

To obtain answers to this question, I asked those who had lost the connection with their families in some way or another. In particular, I sought answers from those who had successfully managed to deal with their situation. A posting to the support groups on the Internet brought numerous responses and suggestions which I will share with you.

First, the consistent suggestion in a number of messages I received was to learn to be your own best friend. This meant learning to nurture and accept yourself and to develop the ability to be alone as well as to be able to reach out to others. It is easier to attract new friends when one has a sense of competence and confidence. Secondly, friends and support groups were considered to be the next source of support and a place to give. We also need connection among our friends. Having friends that know each other exponentially increases our sense of connectivity and allows us to experience a sense of community with our friends.

With regard to friendships, there were some special ideas that facilitated a sense of support. Some suggested that developing two or three close friendships was much better than having a number of acquaintances. Secondly, doing volunteer work that focused on relationships was very rewarding. Some suggested becoming a school volunteer, a scout leader or a big brother or sister as ways of developing meaningful relationships in which we are giving support to others. Church was also suggested as a means of becoming involved in a community. The key to volunteer success was to join an organization that focused on relationships or team work to accomplish the organizational goals.

One technique to combat loneliness and lack of family can be the development of friendship rituals. Much of what families do together consists of rituals such as sharing a meal or watching a movie. Even family day trips involve a series of rituals of preparation. One of the comforts I had in the last city I lived in involved going out for springs rolls and hot and sour soup with my friend Cathy. We would do this on a fairly regular basis and talk about the things that were going on in our lives. Since moving, I have developed other rituals such as going for a steamed milk with my friend Bruce. I have had to recognize the loss of my ritual with Cathy. Rituals seem to provide a structure for the sharing of personal stories, laughter and companionship.

As I found in posing my question, another form of ritual can involve regular reading and posting to the Internet support groups, giving a sense of being part of an on-line community. I made contact with numerous people scattered across North America in my endeavor to obtain a solution to my problem. One user even posted a message adopting me as a group member! I experienced a substantial amount of warmth and encouragement from these people. Similarly, attending a support group can bring relief to loneliness through the sharing of strengths, problems and experience. Groups are often accepting of newcomers. It is also possible to connect with similar groups when traveling or when moving to a new city. Involvement in a 12-step group can often mean that we never have to be alone with our problems, since groups exist in almost every town or city in the world.

It is important to recognize that pursuing a goal of bettering ourselves or others can be more rewarding than solely pursuing a goal of finding a place in which we can belong. The search for belonging often leads us on a path of disappointment when we are let down by the human nature of people's shortcomings. Trying to find a place to belong can often heighten our sense of loneliness and isolation. Achieving a sense of self-worth and developing the ability to be happy and satisfied in meager times can be a powerful ally against loneliness and depression.

The Role of Grieving

As mentioned earlier, grief can be a very isolating emotion. During a period of grief, others may not know what to say to us. We may be lost in a rainbow of emotions. While others may mean well by telling us they know how we feel, we often feel isolated by such comments. Grief that goes unresolved can have a long term impact on our ability to attract and build friendships. As I began my own grief work, I found that people became more open with me as I became more open with them. As I worked through the emotions I had long repressed, others began to feel more comfortable and relaxed around me. Some confided that I had been giving the impression that I wanted to be left alone - the exact opposite of what I really wanted. Unresolved grief can mask itself as depression, particularly if it has been carried for a long time. Obviously then, resolving grief can lead to greater openness and connectedness with others. It has often been said that time is a great healer, but it is not true if we avoid the grieving process.

In particular, the grieving process may also mean coming to terms with the abuse and harm we may have suffered from deceased family members. For the longest time I had the greatest contempt for the shortcomings of my father and the hurtful things that my mother had done. Although my parents had been dead for 10 years, I still carry them with me in my thoughts and these thought still impact how I feel about myself. My unresolved anger towards my parents was still impacting my daily enjoyment of life and the notion of having emotionally abusive, hindering parents was contributing to my sense of loneliness.

It was while doing some work as a web page designer that I came across some research on child bereavement that was very helpful in dealing with my loneliness. A study had shown that children who had lost a parent fared better if they were able to maintain a positive emotional attachment to the deceased parent, while at the same time accepting the loss of the parent. Although this may seem contradictory -that we need to hold on to a part of them yet still let go, it has actually made a great deal of sense to me. Since coming across the research, I have learned to reconcile my own internal representation of my parents.

Previously, I had focused mostly on the negative characteristics of my parents. As I realized that my view was tainted by my anger, I came to see them as humans with shortcomings who did in fact love me, although they had great difficulty showing it. In a sense, I realized that I had to do some forgiving, and to realize that I was angry because they had, in a very real sense, left me. Instead of maintaining a negative internalized image of my parents, I have begun to focus on the ways that they did try to show they loved my. I remember being told by a friend of my father that he often told her how much he loved his five sons. My mother's last message to us before she died, was to "tell the boys that I love them, and that God always comes through". There were times as well when my parent did show that they cared.

While attending a support meeting, I was deeply moved by the words of the son of a long time member who had recently passed away. The man's son believed that, although his father definitely had problems, in dying his father experienced recovery. I am now secure in knowing that my own parents are now free of their pain and issues. They are now free to love me in a manner that was difficult for them when they were alive. Due to my healing process, I am also more free to love them. My internal representation of them has changed.

By recognizing the times that my parents did show love and were nurturing, I have been able to develop a more positive image of my parents. This new image of my parents seems to provide a greater sense of warmth thus lessening my sense of loneliness. As the research suggested, developing an maintaining a positive internal emotional attachment has helped. As in transactional analysis, perhaps those of us who do not have close contact with nurturing parents or siblings can develop our own internal images of nurturing parents.

Nurturing Oneself

During times of emotional pain and healing it is important to give ourselves a break every now and then. Find something that soothes you, be it a favorite work of music, a warm bath, a massage, or reading a good book. Some people I know have even curled up in bed with a teddy bear! The point is that we need times to relax and bring down our stress level. These are important tips to follow even when we are emotionally healthy!

With the stress of a graduate program and the fact that I moved to a new city, I have for the past few months found myself stressed out and needing a recharge. My head is so full of the things that I have to do that I feel overwhelmed. When a friend said to me "what do you do to soothe yourself?", I came up short without any answers. I have since learned that my stress level gets lowered when I set aside some time for relaxation time - even if it is only a few minutes. During this time, I do one or two things that I have discovered to be soothing behaviors. I sing, play my guitar or spend time with my cat. Of course, the behaviors that we find soothing are personal. The things we find soothing may reflect our own interests and hobbies. Try to develop a sense of what works for you. Feel free to suggest your own ideas!

Learn to Put Your Problems Away

Often we need a break from our problems. We may also need to calm ourselves and stop worrying. A wonderful technique to bring this about is to imagine putting each of our problems, one by one, into a strong wooden chest. We then imagine locking the chest with a strong padlock and dropping the chest off a ship into the deepest ocean.

This technique serves as a ceremony for putting our troubles away and helps to reduce our amount of worry. It is healthy because we are not denying that our problems exist, we are simply giving ourselves a break from needless worry.

Eat Well, Rest Well, Exercise Well

At any time in your life, it is a good practice to eat well, get some exercise and rest appropriately. This is also very true during the healing process. Select your groceries well and prepare nutritious meals for yourself. Schedule some rest time during the day, and try to exercise even if it's only moderately. It will help you immensely to maintain better health during and after this process.

Create a Safe Place for Yourself

Most of us do not feel comfortable expressing our emotions in public and society has not yet come to accept open expression of emotions. Perhaps this will come one day, however for the moment we may wish to follow the norms of society. We may not wish to force ourselves to express emotions in front of others, but we will at least wish to be able to feel and express our emotions in the privacy of our home so that we may heal and move on.

Sometimes we may begin to experience an emotion which we want to release. How do we do so with people around? Once I was at a campground and another gentleman and I began discussing getting in touch with feelings. He expressed that he wished he had a place to go and cry. The solution was quite simple. He went for a walk along the road and found a quiet place for himself. In many cases we too can find a safe place when we need to. It could simply be in our car, an office washroom, or a room with a closed door where no one will bother us.

Important to healing is the ability to have a place where you can relax and feel free to express yourself. This may be a room in your house -your bedroom, for example. It should be a place where you can ensure that no one will disturb you if that is your wish. This can be achieved by simply putting a "do not disturb" sign on your door. It's nice to have a few amenities like a soft pillow, a candle for meditating and a journal for writing. Decorate the room with things you cherish. Try to have this room available whenever you need it, so that if you need to release, you can do it on your own timetable.

Create a 'Bad Hair Day' List

Often we have difficult days. Unexpected things happen, we simply wake up on the wrong side of the bed, or as the popu-

Mark Linden O'Meara

lar phrase goes, we have a "bad hair day"! On these days it is helpful to resort to a list you have created on one of your better days. At a time when you are making progress in your recovery, write down the things that you have accomplished, the things that you enjoy, and the things that cheer you up. Perhaps you can make a list of your accomplishments or the things you like about yourself. Put the list in a place where you know you can find it. When you experience one of those "bad hair days", take out the list and do one or more of the things that cheer you up, notice the things that you have made progress in, and give yourself credit for the work you have done!

Validate your Feelings

Many people try to get their feelings and emotions validated by others. Our emotions are our own and others may react differently to them. If we seek validation of our feelings from others, then we give up our personal power and self-esteem to others. If we are feeling a certain way, then these feelings are valid simply because we are having them.

Visualization and Scaling

Visualization can be an effective method of reducing stress and anxiety, especially when combined with a technique called scaling. Imagine on a scale of one to 10 how stressed you are. Then imagine what it would be like to feel half a point lower. Again imagine what it would feel like to feel another half point less stressed. Repeat this process until you have lowered the scale. See if you feel more relaxed. Chances are you will. This is an effective technique that can work for a number of problems and issues. If you are feeling disconnected and ungrounded, the technique can be used in reverse to gain a sense of serenity. Simply reverse the process and imagine what it would feel like to be half a point higher on the scale. Again repeat the process, raising your level by half or full points.

Deep Breathing

One of the first things that a vocal instructor focuses on with the student is proper breathing techniques. When stressed, many of us resort to shallow chest breathing and as a result, we do not experience the rejuvenating benefits of deep abdominal breathing. I have learned a few easy exercises to take in and expel a deep breath, which is the foundation of many yoga exercises.

The exercise I recommend involves lying face down on the floor. Take in a deep breath and notice that your stomach muscles should be pressing against the floor. As you exhale, imagine your diaphragm expelling the air and moving up into your back towards your spine. Then relax and let the air flow in. Practicing this exercise will help you connect with deep diaphragm breathing. Once you know how to do it, you will be able to practice it in any position. I am often amazed at how a few moments of deep breathing can rejuvenate my energy level and reduce my stress level.

Plan Some Rest Time

Of course, just as many of us have different interests, the things we do to relax vary as well. Since I did not want to list only my soothing behaviors, I posted a message on the Internet asking people what soothing things they did. Here are some of the suggestions:

- gardening: transplanting, feeding, watering and nurturing
- playing a musical instrument
- playing with a pet (pets are non-judgmental)
- singing
- listening to music without lyrics
- listening to music with lyrics
- talking to a (real) best friend
- drawing
- a warm bath, with the bathroom lit by candles
- reading newsgroups and web pages on the Internet
- watching a favorite TV show or movie with a friend or pet
- lie on a blanket in the backyard or park with a book
- go to the library, bookstore, arboretum, museum or art gallery
- cook or bake
- read a good book

- journalling
- drink a cup of tea, hot chocolate or steamed milk
- exercise (even just walking is fine)
- volunteer at a place that provides a sense of community
- make a list of things you like about yourself
- get away to nature
- cuddle up with a teddy bear
- have some chocolate (this was a common response!)

Often we need a break from our emotional work. We do not need to spend all of our time working out our pain or dealing with our issues. We need to find healthy distractions that will allow us to recharge. Meditation, theatre, a hobby, or socializing can be as much a part of our healing and renewal process. Read a book, rent a movie, talk to a friend, or listen to some music. We may need to learn to try putting aside our problems for a day or to have a vacation from them. It is OK to turn away from our pain until we are ready to deal with it. Most importantly, have a sense of humor!

Conclusion

In reading this book I hope that you have been able to develop some new attitudes and skills for dealing with and accepting emotions in ourselves and others. Emotional work is a lifelong commitment. It is something we do for ourselves and for our relationship with others in the world. Many of us have had a difficult family upbringing or have experienced difficult times in our lives that, unless resolved, will continue to affect our behavior in subtle and sometimes not so subtle ways.

Through the healing and acceptance of our emotions we can break the cycle of abuse to which we have been subjected. Fortunately, many of us now have the tools to gain greater understanding of ourselves and of others. As adults we can do a better job of ensuring that our unhealthy patterns of behavior and attitudes are not passed on to our children. We can become more loving and responsive to their needs and our own needs as well. Too often it is easier to hate and hold resentment than to forgive.

To work on our emotions and to resolve them brings us freedom - freedom to enjoy life more, to have closer and more trusting relationships and, most importantly, to have clarity of thinking when resolving problems and issues. All of these benefits will allow us to become better friends, teachers and parents.

As we heal we are allowing greater opportunities for ourselves and for others. Through emotional resolution we lift ourselves above the habitual patterns that may have existed in our families for years without our knowing. We can bring about change and greater awareness. We will be better able to accept emotional expression in others. All of these benefits will allow us to foster creativity and more effectively nurture others. Perhaps in the future it won't hurt as much to be human.

"I am not afraid of storms anymore, for I am learning to sail my ship."

- Louisa May Alcott

Bibliography

American Journal of Dance Therapy, Dance/Movement Therapy with Battered Women: A Paradigm of Action, Fall-Win Vol. 13(2) 131-145, 1991

American Journal of Psychology, Crying, 17, 1906

A.F. Ax, The Physiological Differentiation Between Fear and Anger in Humans, Psychosomatic Medicine 15:433 - 442, 1953

Richard P. Benthal, A Proposal to Classify Happiness as a Psychiatric Disorder, Journal of Medical Ethics, Liverpool University

Borquist, A. Crying, American Journal of Psychology , 1906, 17, 149 -205,

Beutler and Engle, Inability to Express Intense Affect: A common link between depression and pain, Journal of Consulting and Clinical Psychology, 1986, Dec Vol 54 (6)

Claudia Black, It's Never Too Late to Have a Happy Childhood, M.A.C. Printing and Publishing. Div. Denver Colorado, 1989

Claudia Black, It Could Never Happen to Me, M.A.C. Printing and Publishing, Denver Colorado. 1982

Boris Blai Jr. Ph.D. Health Consequences of Loneliness: A review of the Literature, Journal of American College Health, 37, 162-167

John Briere Ph.D., Therapy for Adults Molested as Children - Beyond Survival, Springer Publishing Company, New York, 1989

Briere J. and Conte J., Self-reported Amnesia for Abuse in Adults Molested as Children, Journal of Traumatic Stress, 6, 21-31, 1993

Brown University Long-term Care Quality Letter, Tears Not Always a Sign Elderly are Depressed. Dec 22, 1993.

Brown University Long-term Care Quality Letter, The Release of Tears: The first phase in the psychotherapy of a 3-year-old child with the diagnosis: Symbiotic Child Psychosis, International Review of Psycho Analysis, 1980 Vol 7 (3)

David D. Burns, M.D., The Feeling Good Handbook, Penguin Group, ISBN 0-452-26174-0, 1990.

Melba Colgrove, Ph. D., Harold H. Bloomfield, M.D. and Peter McWilliams, How to Survive the Loss of A Love, Prelude Press, Los Angeles California, Bantam Books, ISBN 0-553-07760-0, 1991

Norman Cousins, Anatomy of an Illness, New England Journal of Medicine, 295(26): 1458 - 1463, 1976

Cutrona Ce, Transition to college: Loneliness and the process of social adjustment, in Peplau LA, Perlman D (eds), Loneliness: A

Sourcebook of Current Theory, Research and Therapy, New York, Wiley-Interscience, 1982.

Penelope. J. Davis, Physiological and Subjective Effects of Catharsis: A Case Report

Frederick F. Flach M.D., The Secret Strength of Depression, Bantam Books, ISBN -0-397-01031-1, 1974

Dr. Susan Forward, Toxic Parents, Overcoming Their Hurtful Legacy and Reclaiming Your Life, Bantam Books, ISBN 0-553-28434-7, 1989

Frey, W.H., DeSota-Johnson, D., Hoffman, C and McCall, J.T., Effect of Stimulus on the Chemical Composition of Tears, American Journal of Ophthalmology, 92(4) 1981, 559-67

Gallop G.A. A study to determine the effectiveness of social skills training process in reducing perceived loneliness of social isolation. Doctoral dissertation, Ohio University, 1980.

Judith Ginzberg, In Search of a Voice: Working with Homeless Men, American Journal of Dance Therapy, 1991, Spr-Sum Vol 13(1) 33-48.

Gerald W. Grumet, Laughter: Nature's Epileptoid Catharsis, Psychological Reports, 1989 Dec Vol 65 (3,Pt 2) 1989

Jane Harte, Psychoneuroendocrine Concomitants of the Emotional Experience Associated with Running and Meditation, in Behavior and Immunity, edited by Alan J. Husband. CRC Press, ISBN 0-8493-0199-8

Lou Heber, Dance Movement: A therapeutic program for Psychiatric clients. Perspectives in Psychiatric Care; 1993 Apr-Jun Vol 29(2) 22-29.

Heller K., The Effects of Social Support: Prevention and Treatment Implications, in Goldstein AP, Kanfer FH (eds), Maximizing Treatment Gains: Transfer Enhancement in Psychotherapy. New York, Academic Press, 1979

Judith Lewis Herman, M.D., J Christopher Perry, M.P.H., M.D. and Bessel A. van der Kolk M.D., Childhood Trauma in Borderline Personality Disorder, American Journal of Psychiatry April 1989

Harvey Jackins, Fundamentals of Co-counselling Manual, Personal Counselors Inc., Rational Island Publishers, Seattle, Washington, 1982

Pierre Janet, L'automatisme psychologique, Paris, 1889

Lynn Johnson, Creative Therapies in the Treatment of Addictions: The Art of Transforming Shame, Arts in Psychotherapy, 1990 Win Vol 17(4) 299-308.

Kassel, Jon D., Wagner Eric, F. Processes of Change in Alcoholics Anonymous: A Review of Possible Mechanisms, Psychotherapy, Vol 30 (2), 1993

Anna Kaye and Don C. Matchan, Mirror of the Body, Strawberry Hill Press, San Francisco, California., 1978

C. Kristiansen, K. Felton, W. Hovdestad, C. Allard, Ottawa Survivor's Study: A Summary of Findings, Carleton University, 1995

Dr. Kevin Leman and Randy Carlson, Unlocking the Secrets of Your Childhood Memories. Thomas Nelson Publishers. ISBN 0-8407-7631-4, 1989

Lohnes, K.L. and Kalter, N., Preventive Intervention Groups for Parentally Bereaved Children. American Journal of Orthopsychiatry: 1994, 64(4):594-603.

James J. Lynch, The Broken Heart: The Psychobiology of Human Contact, The Healing Brain - A Scientific Reader, Edited by Robert Ornstein and Charles Swencionis, Guilford Press, ISBN 0-89862-394-4, 1990

Mechanic D., Social structure and personal adaptation: Some neglected dimensions, in Coelho GU, Hamburg D.A., Adam J.E. (eds), Coping and Adaptation. New York , Basic Books, 1974.

Dr. Rod McCormick, The Facilitation of Healing Among First Nations People of British Columbia, Doctoral Dissertation, University of British Columbia, 1994

Thomas Moore, Care of The Soul: A guide for cultivating depth and sacredness in everyday life, Harper-Collins Publishers, New York, 1992

Robert Ornstein and David S. Sobel, The Brain as a Health Maintenance Organization, The Healing Brain - A Scientific Reader, Edited by Robert Ornstein and Charles Swencionis, Guilford Press, ISBN 0-89862-394-4, 1990

Robert Ornstein, Ph.D. and David Sobel, M.D, Healthy Pleasures, Addison-Wesley Publishing Co. ISBN 0-201-12669-9 1989

Norman Vincent Peale, The Power of Positive Thinking, Fawcett Publications Inc. Greenwich, Conn., 1952

Frederick S. Perls M.D., Ph.D., Gestalt Theory Verbatim, Real People Press, Lafayette, California, 1969

Rubenstein C, Shaver P., In Search of Intimacy. New York, Delacourt, 1982

Erika Saunders, Letter of the Day, Ottawa Citizen, October 5, 1995 page A14,

T.J. Scheff, Catharsis in Healing, Ritual and Drama, University of California Press, Berkeley and Los Angeles, California, 1979

Gordon F. Shea, Managing a Difficult or Hostile Audience,

Prentice-Hall, Englwood Cliffs, New Jersey, 1984

Andrew Slaby MD., Phd., M.P.H., Aftershock: Surviving the Delayed Effects of Trauma, Crisis and Loss, Fair Oaks Press, Villard Books, Random House, 1989

Lenore Terr, M.D., Unchained Memories: True Stories of Traumatic Memories, Lost and Found, Basic Books, ISBN 0-465-08823-6, 1994

Bessel A. Van der Kolk, Rita Fisler, Dissociation and the Fragmentary Nature of Traumatic Memories: Overview and Exploratory Study, Harvard Medical School, Department of Psychiatry

Bessel A. Van der Kolk, The Body Keeps the Score: Memory and the Evolving Psychobiology of Posttraumatic Stress. Harvard Review of Psychiatry, Jan-Feb 1994 Vol 1 No 5, 253-265.

Appendix A -Resources

The following is a list of resources on the Internet that may be helpful to you. In addition, you can likely obtain listings of support groups and other resources from organizations in your community. Most city telephone directories list contact numbers for 12-step groups. Community health center may also have resources or they may be able to refer you to the appropriate organization.

Since the content of the Internet changes rapidly, the addresses shown below may change. Use your search engine to identify new addresses or new sites.

List of Usenet Support Newsgroups:

Following is a list of Usenet Support Groups. In addition to the list below, there are also numerous groups dedicated to the support of various medical problems. To access, use your newsgroup reader. Use the "add newsgroup" command and type in the name of the newsgroup. It is not mandatory to post to these groups. Simply reading the postings is perfectly acceptable and can provide insight and support.

Alt.Abuse...
alt.abuse-recovery
alt.abuse.offender.recovery
alt.abuse.transcendence

Alt.Psychology...
alt.psychology.help
alt.psychology.mindmachine - (effects of light/sound technology)
alt.psychology.synchronicity
alt.psychology.transpersonal

Alt.Recovery...
Alt.recovery
Alt.recovery.aa

alt.recovery..na
alt.recovery.addiction.gambling
alt.recovery.addiction.sexual
alt.recovery.adult-children
alt.recovery.catholicism
alt.recovery.codependence
alt.recovery.compulsive-eat
alt.recovery.nicotine
alt.recovery.panic-anxiety.self-help
alt.recovery.religion
alt.sexual.abuse.recovery
alt.abuse.recovery
alt.irc.recovery
alt.usenet.recovery

Alt.Support...
alt.support
alt.support.abortion
alt.support.abuse-partners
alt.support.aids.partners
alt.support.anxiety-panic
alt.support.chronic-pain
alt.support.depression
alt.support.depression.manic
alt.support.depression.family
alt.support.depression.misc
alt.support.depression.treatment
alt.support.dissociation
alt.support.divorce
alt.support.eating-disord
alt.support.emotions
alt.support.ex-cult
alt.support.grief
alt.support.grief.pet-loss
alt.support.loneliness
alt.support.menopause
alt.support.ocd

alt.support.shyness
alt.support.single-parents
alt.support.survivors.prozac
alt.support.trauma-ptsd
soc.support.youth.gay-lesbian-bi
alt.self-improve
alt.med.fybromyalgia

Web Pages of Interest

Psyberspace-etc
A comprehensive guide to Internet mental health and healing information, with links to the pages listed below, lists of support newsgroups, and other resources. Links to professional association and online 12 step groups. Reviews and comments on Here I Am as well as ordering information.
http://www3.bc.sympatico.ca/soulcare

GriefNet
A collection of resources of value to those who are experiencing loss and grief, is sponsored by Rivendell Resources, a non-profit foundation based in Ann Arbor, USA.
http://www.rivendell.org

David Baldwin's Trauma Info Pages.
A comprehensive resource for the treatment of emotional trauma and traumatic stress, including Post-traumatic Stress Disorder. Topic areas here range from Trauma Resources, to General Support, to Disaster Mental Health Handouts. There are links from these pages to related issues and disorders such as addiction, anxiety and panic, domestic violence, and grief.
http://www.trauma-pages.com

Adult Chidren Anonymous (ACA)
ACA (ACoA) is a 12 Step, 12 Tradition Fellowship for people who grew up in Alcoholic or Dysfunctional families.
http://www.AdultChildren.org/

Dr. John Grohol's Mental Health Page
Dr. Grohol's pages are a one-stop index for psychology, support, and mental health issues, resources, and people on the Internet. Contains links for newsgroups, mailing lists, book reviews and chat services on the Net.
http://www.grohol.com/

Alanon and Alateen
Are you or have you been affected by the actions of a drinker? Need support? Find out about the assistance available from Alanon and Alateen.
http://www.Al-anon-Alateen.org

Alcohohics Anonymous
Official site of the AA organization. Find out about their philosophy and how you can begin to help yourself. Locate a meeting in your area.
http://www.alcoholics-anonymous.org/

Emotions Anonymous is a twelve-step organization, similar to Alcoholics Anonymous. It is a fellowship is composed of people who come together in weekly meetings for the purpose of working toward recovery from emotional difficulties.
http://www.mtn.org/EA

Mental Health Net
Mental Health Net, is a large, comprehensive guide to mental health online, featuring over 6,000 individual resources. The award-winning fun & friendly site covers information on disorders such as depression, anxiety, panic attacks, chronic fatigue syndrome and substance abuse, to professional resources in psychology, psychiatry and social work, journals and self-help magazines.
http://www.cmhc.com/

Mark Linden O'Meara

Virtual Pamphlet Collection
Student counseling centers often educate through informational
pamphlets on various topics. This page contains a collection of
very informative virtual pamphlets on a variety of topics.
http://uhs.bsd.uchicago.edu/scrs/vpc/vpc.

Tom Golden's Crisis, Grief and Healing Page
This page is meant to be a place men and women can browse to
understand and honor the many different paths to heal strong emotions.
http://www.webhealing.com/

Mental Health Net
Mental Health Net, is a large, comprehensive guide to mental health
online, featuring over 6,000 individual resources. The award-winning fun & friendly site covers information on disorders such as
depression, anxiety, panic attacks, chronic fatigue syndrome and
substance abuse, to professional resources in psychology, psychiatry and social work, journals and self-help magazines.
http://www.cmhc.com/

Index

For additional copies of "Here I Am: Finding Oneself Through Healing and Letting Go", please photocopy and complete the following order form and send it with payment to:

Soul Care Publishing
1733 H Street, Suite 330-965
Blaine, WA
98230-5106

Please send _____ copies @ $12.95 U.S./ $16.95 Cdn

Total for books $_____
Add: Postage and Handling:
    $2.00 per book: _____
TOTAL: $_____

Please bill my   Visa __   Mastercard __

Card No: _____ Expiry __/__

Name on Card: _____

Signature _____

Ship to:
Name:_____
Address:_____
City:_____ State:_____
Zip Code:_____
Telephone: (   ) _____ - _____

_____
Please make cheques or money orders payable to
Soul Care Publishing. Do not send cash in the mail.